Behind Enemy Lines

The OSS in World War II

One Small Part

Al Johnson

Printed in the United States of America 3

Style Publishing
4356 Blackfoot Dr. SW
Grandville MI 49418
markvws@yahoo.com

Dedication

This story is dedicated to the men of OSS Group "Patrick" and O.G. Command Group "Blueberry"; both of which served their country well behind enemy lines. The story as I saw and experienced it. There are probably many little instances that occurred, but were not recorded because of a lapse of time or a laps of memory. Also, this is dedicated to my grandchildren who kept after me to tell them what I had done during the Second World War.

A special thanks is given to Larry Drew and Jim Gardner for their input into this story, and also to Roy Gallant who became a special friend while fighting in the field.

Office of Strategic Services

A 20 year old Al Johnson in Kunming, China

The French Legion of Honor Medal
Created by Napoleon, the highest honor France can bestow

Al Johnson at 87

CONTENTS

A Short History of the
Office of Strategic Services OSS

Before 1940, the U.S. State Department, FBI and the different branches of the military all had their own security and counterintelligence operations, which did not easily share information with each other. With another war raging in Europe, however, President Franklin D. Roosevelt wanted greater coordination when it came to gathering and acting on intelligence. In July 1941, he tapped Colonel William J. Donovan, known as "Wild Bill," for a newly created office, Coordinator of Information (COI).

Donovan, who served as a battalion commander in the 165th Infantry Regiment during World War I, was one of the nation's most decorated war heroes. As he began laying the groundwork for a coordinated intelligence network, based partially on the example of the British Secret Intelligence Service (MI6), the new COI office provoked suspicion and hostility from other U.S. agencies, including J. Edgar Hoover's FBI and the War Department's Military Intelligence Division, better known as the G-2.

After the Japanese attack on Pearl Harbor, Roosevelt acted swiftly to improve U.S. intelligence capabilities even further. In June of 1942, the President issued an executive order establishing the OSS, which replaced the COI and was charged with collecting and analyzing strategic intelligence and running special operations outside the other branches of the U.S. military, under the control of the Joint Chiefs of Staff. As head of the OSS, Donovan was frustrated when his rival agencies effectively blocked access to intercepted Axis communication, the most vital source of wartime intelligence.

Despite such obstacles, Donovan quickly built up the ranks of his organization, training new recruits in national parks in Maryland and Virginia and establishing full-fledged operations in Europe, Asia and elsewhere. In addition to gathering intelligence, fostering resistance and spreading disinformation behind enemy lines, OSS operatives carried out soldier rescues, guerilla warfare and sabotage, among other missions. The organization also developed its own counterintelligence operation, known as the X-2 branch, which could operate overseas but had no jurisdiction in the Western Hemisphere.

Before Operation TORCH, the Allied invasion of North Africa in late 1942, a dozen OSS officers traveled to the region and worked as "vice consuls" in several ports, establishing local networks and gathering information that would prove vital to the successful Allied landings. In advance of the D-Day landings in Normandy in 1944, paratroopers in the Special Operations (SO) branch of the OSS parachuted into Nazi-occupied France, Belgium and the Netherlands to coordinate air drops of supplies, meet up with local resistance forces and make guerrilla attacks on German troops. As Dwight D. Eisenhower once said of the OSS: "If (it) had done nothing else, the intelligence gathered alone before D-Day justified its existence." With the defeat of Germany, some OSS soldiers returned to the United States for additional training before being redeployed to the China-Burma India theater where they undertook the task of training Chinese guerrillas for combat against the Japanese.

Roosevelt died in April 1945, and his successor Harry S. Truman had no inclination to prolong the existence of the OSS when World War II ended later that year. By executive order, Donovan's agency was dissolved as of October 1945, but its secret Intelligence (SI) and X-2 branches would become the nucleus of a new peacetime intelligence service, the Central Intelligence Agency (CIA), created in 1947. The OSS is also credited for being the forerunner of the Special Forces divisions in each of the branches of the Armed Services.

At its peak, in late 1944, nearly 13,000 men and women had worked for the OSS, with some 7,500 of these deployed overseas. Their identities remained classified until 2008, when the National Archives released OSS personnel records. In addition to four CIA directors— Allen Dulles, Richard Helms, William Colby and William Casey—the ranks of the OSS had included U.S. Supreme Court Justice Arthur Goldberg, Pulitzer Prize-winning historian Arthur Schlesinger Jr., film director John Ford, actor Sterling Hayden, Harvard scholar Ralph Bunche (the first African-American recipient of the Nobel Peace Prize) and baseball player and coach Moe Berg. We can also include Al Johnson.

Behind Enemy Lines

ONE SMALL PART

Chapter 1

There are five of us in the belly of the B-24 Bomber, parachutes on, gear and side arms in place. Our rifles are secured in the containers in the bomb bay. We aren't the only plane heading for France; four other B-24's are in the formation. We are all at 10,000 feet headed for the drop zone into our assigned area at Eguzon, France, 400 miles behind German lines. Our assignment - to work with the French Underground, called the Maquis of F.F.I. [French Forces of the Interior]; first, to capture a hydro-electric plant, then to harass the Germans, and also to collect intelligence to be radioed back to London Headquarters. The French are expecting us because our contact has been there for several months making plans to receive us. His code name is "Hugh". It was the night of August 14th, 1944 and we had been sent to spearhead operation "Anvil" - the southern invasion of France.

It seemed a tremendous assignment! All of this was heaped upon us at the last minute. We had taken our training well, had done all of the things required of us and had actually enjoyed the commando training, relishing our physical contact in simulated attacks. Now, as we were flying in, came the realization that we would have to put all of this into practice.

With time to think, my mind went back to Denver, Colorado. I was sitting in a holding camp awaiting assignment to an outfit, when a notice was placed on the bulletin board about a need for volunteers for a dangerous assignment. Waiting around was not very dangerous, and so the bulletin announcement sounded like something I should try. The list was long but I was friendly with the First Sergeant in the camp and he placed my name on the top of the list. This proved to be a big help. It so happened that only twelve were needed and because of the need for speed the first twelve were taken. We all had the same qualifications -- we were medics. We had never heard of the O.S.S., but were interested in getting into an outfit that would see some action. After many questions were asked, we were taken into the squad leader's office in the barracks and were interviewed by an Officer from O.S.S. We were told to get our things together and report in front, ready to be sent away.

It is interesting to look back to see how your life takes twists and turns. My disappointment at being a medic was great, but as I am flying along to meet the enemy I decided that I had had good training; not only as a medic to save lives, but as an underground agent to take lives, if necessary.

Upon being drafted, I was sent to Ft. Custer in Battle Creek., Michigan. All the men I went down with were immediately assigned to units of the army. I was put to work in the post office. It seemed like a good job, but it wasn't long before I discovered myself enroute to Abeline, Texas for basic training. The next six weeks were spent in hot, dry, conditions where I learned to march, eat, and think army. I enjoyed it. I had been born in an Army hospital and had spent the first years of my life with a father that was regular army. After these six weeks, I was sent to Ft. Sam Houston in San Antonio, Texas, and ended up at the army hospital there. I found out through aptitude tests that I could apply for surgical training. This I did, and took advantage of all the training I could get. It paid off in the end.

I was disappointed enough at being a medic, and was certainly not going to allow myself to sit out the war in a hospital somewhere, while everyone else I knew was probably in a fighting outfit. If worse came to worse, I knew that surgical training would at least keep out of a ward where I could expect to be no more than a bed-pan jockey. I also knew that I would continue to apply for something else until I could get out of this bad situation I was in.

Before any of us were accepted, our backgrounds were looked into. We had to undergo a thorough investigation by officers from O.S.S. We were asked question about our character and background, and if we spoke, or could learn a foreign language. The questions were fired at us rapidly, and I tried to answer them as honestly as possible. Agents were also sent to our respective home towns to gather information about us. We also had to be cleared by the F.B.I. before we were allowed into the O.S.S.

After arriving in Washington, D.C., those of us from Denver were sent by truck through the back streets to a place called the "Gas Factory". This was an old, seemingly abandoned building, near the heart of downtown that was being used by the O.S.S. as its headquarters. Who ever thought anything important would be taking place in such an old and rundown structure? We entered an alley, and with the lights out on the trucks, we were secreted into the building by means of an outside metal stairway. Trying to keep twelve eager men quiet on metal stairs was not an easy task. We entered a long hall that had the smell of must and disuse. Guarded voices could be heard behind the closed doors that we passed. Soon we entered a large room at the end of the hall and stood in the dimmed lights of the bulbs dangling from the ceiling. We were briefed once again, as to what it meant to join the O.S.S., and asked if any of us would like to back out. They had to be kidding! Not one of us had even considered that possibility! This was too interesting to back out now. After we were sworn in, the same truck that brought us here was ready to take us to Area "F". This, we found out, was the Congressional Country Club, made available to us for our training.

The Congressional Country Club had a large club house that offered many of the original facilities that had been available to congressmen. There was a plush lounge area, fine dining rooms, a large ball room, and exercise and gym facilities on the lower level. The hand ball courts became a place that many of us frequented when our schedules would allow. Dress was informal and rank was very seldom shown, so I became familiar with officers and enlisted men alike. We were all treated equally. Calisthenics and daily 5 mile runs before breakfast, conditioned our bodies and minds to a fine point. This was all important for our future survival behind enemy lines. Weapons training and hand-to-hand combat were taught in the successive weeks and we, in turn, became experts in these fields. Now I was ready, and, I had the added knowledge of medical training to go along with these skills.

The drone of the four engines worked its way into my very inner self and even though sleep was out of the question I became very relaxed. The planes' radio operator asked me if I would care to listen to the B.B.C. I accepted and listened to the London Philharmonic play very pleasing music.

Time slipped by and we approached the moment of

departure. When the call came, we all assumed our positions on the floor of the bomber. In order to parachute from a bomber, the ball turret had been removed before take-off leaving a large hole in the bottom about 60" in diameter. This was overlaid with a piece of plywood so no one would accidentally step into the hole and fall out. When the plywood was removed you could see lights on the ground below. It all happened so soon! The engines slowed and I could feel the plane descend. This was it! No turning back! My mouth turned dry and my pulse quickened. As I sat there waiting for my turn to leave the plane, my mind flashed back to the jump training I had received.

We were sent to Casablanca, North Africa by ship. The ship was the General W.A. Mann, a liberty ship built by Wm. Kaiser. The notable thing about this ship was that it rolled continuously. I believe it even rolled in port on smooth water. The trip was almost 30 days in length, as we had to zigzag in order to avoid being spotted by submarines. The entire convoy was slow, as we could go no faster than the slowest vessel.

After arriving, we were transferred by rail car to Guietville, Algeirs in North Africa. This was the first week of April, 1944. It took us about 8 days -- heading eastward across the Atlas Mountains, through Oran, Sidi-Bel Adess and finally arriving in Guietville, a small town just east of Algiers. All of us had looked forward to a short visit in Casablanca. This is the city we had heard of from the movie with Humphrey Bogart; a mysterious city that held all of the intrigue of the African coast - ancient houses and cafe's with dark figures lurking in doorways - brightly lit cafes and people from all parts of the world mingling together over drinks and strange food. Boy, did we want to visit the heart of Casablanca! The city was off limits, but that would not have mattered to us. We all would have left our command and gone to town except for one thing, we were immediately shipped out and on our way to Algiers.

I remember arriving in Algiers. The town was laid out on a hillside that glided down to the sea. For protection, this was probably a common thing to do. Rows and rows of houses and buildings seemed stacked on top of each other, all gazing out to the Mediterranean Sea. A long wide stairway worked its way from the docks up through the city of buildings that reached the very top of the hill. It was a magnificent sight that could only be appreciated first hand. It was unfortunate that I could not spend more time exploring this ancient city, but the training we were to go through prevented me from doing this.

The rail cars we used to get there were old 40 and 8 boxcars used during the First World War. Boy, it was a rotten trip! C-rations were issued us, but we supplemented our diet by the purchase of bread and wine along the way. An order had been issued that we could not leave the train at the little towns we stopped at. This order did not bother us as we made our way to the areas where we could bring the local cuisine. Guietville was to be our home until we learned to parachute. It was originally intended that we learn the art of parachuting at Ft. Benning, Ga., but because of the need to get us overseas the place chosen was a school run by Benning personnel. This provided the O.S.S. with the option of sending us to France or Italy from this point. There were Italian groups with us as well, and they stayed on after we were sent to England.

We were again put through strenuous physical training. We were housed in tents for the first time that many of us could remember. Local Algerians were hired to do the menial tasks of preparing our meals and housekeeping duties. We were in intensive training because time was moving fast and the war needed our expertise. New types of physical training were started and some of the more difficult ones involved the use of ropes. These were attached to high poles and we had to climb them hand over hand to the top. From there we scaled a wall and would be required to drop to the other side without breaking bones or damaging ourselves in another way. After all of this additional training was completed we were sent to a small field that seemed hardly large enough to accommodate a C-47 airplane; nevertheless, we became airborne and took off flying over the Mediterranean Sea. The area for our practice drops was close to the shoreline and it seemed we would land in the sea each time we left the plane. None of us ever did ditch in the water, but it was always on our minds. After our last qualifying jump we were awarded our wings and diplomas. Pride swelled in our breasts as the base commander pinned on our wings.

The wind from the slip stream rushed past my ears as my feet carried me out of the hole and into complete darkness. In my mind's eye I could see the training I had received in the English Commando School. There they taught me to exit a bomber through the hole left by removing the ball turret of the plane as we were doing in France. Normally, a paratrooper leaves from the side door of a C-47 with a tremendous snap of the chute and harness.

I took a quick look at my watch just before I left the plane and it read 1:20 A.M. - my entry into France on the night of August 14th, 1944. This jump reminded me of practice jumps I had made from a hot air balloon when we took the British Commando training at Ringway Field in England. At that time we were driven to a field that had large balloons attached by 1000 ft. cables to a truck containing a wench. This allowed us to be raised for jumping and could also be retrieved for the next "stick" to occupy and be raised for its jump. In the field were many sheep as well. We were jokingly reminded not to land in any of the sheep dung that covered areas of the ground. It was a beautiful ride, both up by balloon and down by parachute. No noise, no slip stream, just your own heart beat sounding like a sledge hammer vibrating inside your rib cage. Down I came, fully convinced I had taken the fastest trip to suicide! The chute opened and I was brought to reality and the present. As I grabbed my risers I could see the bonfires set in a pattern that allowed us to enter enemy territory. A certain agreed-upon-pattern had to be recognized before we were allowed to jump. The Germans would sometimes build fires in order to intercept a drop. We had to be on the alert for this. I slowly descended to the ground. The height was low, about 500 feet, so it was only a few seconds before I hit the ground. Flying at night, the distance can easily be miss-judged. This was the closest we could jump to the ground without all of us being hurt. It takes about 350 feet to open the chute with a static line, so you can see the remaining distance was speedily traveled. I went into the prescribed and well learned roll. When I had completely stopped I was startled by a figure standing over me. My instant reaction was to get out of my harness and pull my pistol.

"Just relax; you've come to the right place. I'm with the Maquis," the figure told me.

"I'm sure glad to hear you speak English", I responded.

"Are you all right?" He questioned me.

"I'm fine, thanks," was all I could respond.

"Let help you out of your harness so you can go help the others."

He explained to me that he was in the First World War and had stayed in France. He was an American and was working with the underground. I thanked him again, but I never found out what his name was, nor did I recall seeing him again.

After we were assisted by the Maquis, we assembled ourselves to see that everyone had arrived safely. We discovered that only three planes had dropped their cargo and men. This made it necessary for us to hide until the next night, in hopes the planes would return. This could have its problems. The Germans would be curious why three bombers came over so low to the ground. After all, if they were that low they should have crashed. We headed for a near-by woods and waited for the next night to close its darkness around us. We posted sentries around the woods and were assisted by the Marquis, who kept us well concealed. The next night, right on schedule, the two missing planes arrived. We were in place and had the same two bonfire patterns lit. It didn't take long before the rest of the group came down. It wasn't long after that before the French women in the area latched onto the parachutes. They used the materials for under clothing - a commodity sadly lacking in occupied France.

The Maquis were well organized. After all, they had been fighting the Germans for many years already. Our arrival had been the force to unite these people and provide them with weapons and materials to make their fight easier. All of our gear, weapons and supplies were loaded onto trucks. We climbed aboard and off we went into the darkness, headed for a small village by the name of LeBlanc. The trucks we were in had belonged to the Germans. Any needs like transportation or gasoline were stolen by the underground and put to good use.

We also discovered, in the very near future, that the helmets we were issued in England were a detriment to our cause. At night, when most of our travel took place, the helmet had the same silhouette as the German helmet and several times we were shot at by the locals. Fortunately we survived these encounters. The only solution was to purchase berets from the French. DuBois and Harnois, two of our men that spoke fluent French, made a trip into to town to purchase enough head wear for all of us. This did eliminate the problem. Probably some French woman used my helmet to cook beans in ...I never did see it again.

The village of LeBlanc, France appeared before us. The

city was probably no larger than one or two hundred people. With the lights out on the trucks we were going down country roads at a good clip, certainly not at a safe speed. But why be concerned? We had youth on our side and the French as our friends. It never occurred to us to be afraid. Even though the Germans were camped about 5 miles from us, we had the confidence that comes with being young and well trained. It wasn't long before we swung into a yard and we all got out of the three trucks. We had stopped between a small cafe` and a house with a barn in the rear. The Maquis quickly escorted us into the barn and told us to bury ourselves in the hay. This was to be our temporary home until we could make planes to carry out our assignment. The cafe` was a welcome sight. We knew it was a place we could spend a good many hours. We all had sufficient French money, but we found that the people were very generous and did not accept our money in payment for food.

"Get your foot out of my face, you dumb-bell. It's bad enough that I can't breathe", someone complained. Sgt. Dolozal yelled back, "Keep quiet you guys! Don't you know we are close to the Germans? You'll have your chance to be heroes later. Now get some rest." Someone also piped up from the other side of the barn, "I'm sure going to find another place to stay than this barn."

"Shut up and don't snore", commanded Dolozal. This was the beginning of many sleepless nights in many strange places. We were to realize, as time went on, that the barn was to be looked at as a first rate hotel.

The assignment we were given back at Brockhall, Northhampton, England was to capture and hold a hydro-electric plant. I recall sitting in the main hall at Brockhall with those chosen to go into France. This group was called "Patrick". Code names were assigned to each operational group [known as O.G.'s] and ours was known as "Patrick".

The officers and enlisted men were all present. A large map of the area surrounding the hydro-electric plant was displayed on one wall, and the meeting was called to order. Lt. Col. Serge Oblinski, our commanding officer, began to explain our operation. After a verbal explanation and a description were given to us, we were shown pictures of the plant we had to capture. The plant was located on a river that flowed near the city of Eguzon. The river was good sized and so the plant was also good sized. We would be jumping near here at a small town named LeBlanc. A minimum amount of information was given to us about the plant or the surrounding area. Some pictures were passed around but they did not do justice to the actual installation. Maybe this was wise, as we could have been discouraged before we started. I doubt there was one of us that could believe the enormity of the assignment.

I, for one, had never seen a hydro-electric plant and was overwhelmed at its size. I couldn't believe we had to capture it. Us with only 25 men, and at that time an unknown number of French Underground. Hey, we were to be 400 miles from any of our own troops. Well, I had volunteered for this, so I had to make the best of it. I wasn't really afraid as much as I was overcome with the size of the assignment.

We were sworn to secrecy and all leaves were canceled. Our job now was putting together all the things we would need for the operation. One thing needed for sure would be plastic explosives. This was something new the army was working on and we were given the privilege of using it in the field. Several of us were assigned the job of putting together the right sized packages. Working with this stuff proved to be a headache. The plastic explosive was really made up of nitroglycerin, and after working it into packages about the size of a pound of hamburger, it would enter our blood stream and give us a good headache. After a short break we could return to the job until it repeated the process. Hob Miller, Grant Hill, Roy Gallant, Bob

Reppenhagen and I, plus Rudy Dolozal were the ones that got to do most of it. Jim Gardner was away at radio school along with Chuck Cotureaux. Of course, Rudy was our demolition man and it was his responsibility to see that the packages were right.

Brockhall held a lot of memories for us. This is where we spent our time getting to know each other. This is where we worked together and played together. This is where we made bonds that would prove to be necessary when we went into combat. Brockhall was unique in that it was a large manor house that was self-contained. It had its own chapel and cemetery adjacent to the manor. Other out buildings contained a horse barn and storage sheds. They reminded me of country homes in films about England. We were not allowed to visit these areas but I did go through them one time with Capt. Cook. The rooms in Brockhall were all heated by individual fireplaces. One room was set aside for my dispensary and I spent many days there when I had patients in sickbay.

We purchased bicycles in the town of Whedon that provided us with our local transportation. Whedon was a small town about four miles from Brockhall and had several pubs and restaurants. With the help of the young ladies in town we were able to enjoy our evenings. I became friendly with one family and before I jumped into France I gave my bicycle to the man of the family. I knew I would not need it and even upon returning I knew I would be heading home and somewhere else to jump into.

CHAPTER II

After securing ourselves in the small village of LeBlanc, a patrol was sent out to reconnoiter the hydro-electric plant near the city of Eguzon. It wasn't long before the patrol returned and told the rest of us that a small company of Germans, in charge of a Lieutenant, was guarding the place. Our information also told us that the place was surrounded by booby traps, placed there to help the Germans. Fortunately, this bit of information was incorrect. We found that the Germans felt they were secure at that point in the war, and we were most happy to discover that obstacle wasn't present. False information like that could keep the Maquis at bay, as they were constantly harassing the Germans. With inadequate weapons it was not possible to do much damage. With our arrival, heavy weapons were brought into play.

It was now time to take action, so we moved to the Mouhet area, which was well situated for the Maquis Headquarters. This was located in a large woods about 10 miles from our objective and about one quarter mile from the road leading to Paris from Limoges. Since this road was put out of commission by the Maquis, any German movements were compelled to use side roads and detours, which the underground had purposely provided so that ambushes would be set up. This whole plan was carried out within a ten mile radius of our camp.

A meeting was called with the underground soon after our arrival, and plans were made that within two days the Germans would be attacked in their bivouac area. We had a total of about 200 French, including our 25 men. We were about 10 miles from Eguzon, and had to circumvent the city of Argenton which was held by the Germans. This whole area was infested with Germans, small groups of them ... enough to keep the local citizens in line. Because of this we could not travel in a convoy, but had to make our trip in crowded trucks down back roads and cow paths that could be found. Passing through small villages was like a circus entering town. It was obvious the French knew our intent. Since many of the citizens, both male and female, were in the underground, it was understood that the people in the country would know of our work. This had its disadvantages. One distinct plus was that we received information useful to our London office on troop movements and strengths. Sometimes, the desire, on the part of the French peasantry was too great and information from one area did not confirm information from another. It was our duty to accept all and glean what we felt to be true.

When we finally all arrived, we located ourselves in and around the dam, making sure we were not seen. Because there were people that collaborated with the Germans, they knew we were on the way. What we did not want them to know was how many of us there were and where we were located. Our point of arrival, of course, was at the bottom of the hydra plant. From this point we could look up and see the massive structure looming above us. A road wound its way to the top and proceeded across it, finally disappearing in a cover of trees. The road presented the only clear way to the top. Going up the embankment would have been futile. A sensible means had to be thought of in order to take the plant without the loss of lives or the loss of the installation. Even a small number of Germans could have presented a formidable defense if we were to storm the fortifications. This would only constitute foolishness. The base of the plant contained the barracks and administration offices. This was our area of concentration.

Our problem was now complicated because a Captain Clavel, who was commanding the First Regiment of France located at Eguzon, planned to oppose us. The Petan

Government had sent him there to aid the Germans in holding the city, as well as the dam. Col. Oblinski, under a flag of truce, invited the Captain to a meeting. Col. Oblinski said he had orders from General Koeing to the F.F.I. to take the dam as well as the city, and hold it; and would attack with a sizable force of paratroopers and underground. Seeing an American Colonel had a lot to do with Captain Clavel changing his mind, and he agreed that his objectives were the same as ours. It's surprising how weak some of the French had become under their German captors. Colonel Oblinski then suggested that Captain Clavel tell the Germans to leave the dam without a fight. The German Lieutenant must have been impressed, because it wasn't long before they all took off in trucks and cars, leaving behind most of their equipment and personal items. The hydro-electric plant was now in our hands, even though Eguzon was still held by the Germans. The capture of it would come later.

Many of us thought the barracks of the Germans would be a good place to stay. Whoever it was that boasted about staying in a better place than the barn, must have felt good about the barracks. It did look good, better than where we were staying back a LeBlanc. Well, it didn't take long to discover that the German forgot to take along their bedbugs. The place was crawling with them! So, back to our good ol' barn in the nice clean hay and straw.

Before leaving, I made a tour of the office area. Here I discovered a German official stamp with a Swastika and also a sheet of German stamps, unused. These I pocketed, along with a small German banner.

The French that had originally operated the hydro-electric plant were happy to get back to their jobs and take over operation of the plant again. Captain Clavel provided guards for the operation and we left knowing the dam would be secure.

After this, many small incidents took place in which we set up ambushes to slow down German movements and activities in the area. There were always German troops going from one place to the other and the underground would make it difficult for these movements. We were invited to participate whenever we had the desire. This was a constant harassment for the Germans, but the French were enjoying their new found source of ammunition and friends from America. Also, we were constantly sending messages back to London headquarters about these activities so the Allies would have a track on the movements of German troops in the area. A big push was on to withdraw Hitler's troops back to Germany. Also, the fact that the Southern invasion had taken place was another reason the Germans were on the move.

The French captured very few of the enemy. There was no place to keep them and no reason to feed them. By and large the French had had enough of the suppressive yoke of the Germans and were willing to offer a little retaliation of their own. Whatever information could be squeezed out was taken and then the captives were liquidated. On one occasion Captain Cook who headed a squad of men, including myself, stopped at the Maquis headquarters. We were on a reconnaissance patrol. The Maquis had a German officer in camp who had been questioned extensively. The German was surprised to see us and when he did he pleaded for his life. Captain Cook did what he could to prevent the French from doing the very thing the German officer knew would happen. It wasn't long before we heard a shot. War is such a crazy waste of everything!

At the time we were there, we were told of a party of Germans that were in the area. Capt. Cook said, "It would be nice to get this patrol so I can question them. Maybe we can get some information from them that can be used by London."

Rudy Dolozal piped up, "We're ready if you are!"

"O.K.," yelled Cookie, "Take the squad and hop in the truck." With this we were immediately shuttled off to the area.

Captain Cook was a man of great energy and drive. He was not a demanding person, but one that caused you to be very loyal to him. He did not waste a lot of words; when he spoke you knew you had to respond without question. He was eager to find these Germans. Word was given to us on a possible location and we were dropped off on a road across from a Chateau. I believe the name of it was Lussas Les Chateau. The road was not a heavily traveled one and I suppose the Germans were also looking for us. It was more comfortable to be the hunter than the hunted. From this point we spread out through the field surrounding the Chateau following hedgerows and trees. Some areas were quite open and at any time I expected to hear gun fire. None came.

Several of our men went around the left side toward the main entrance of the Chateau. Roy Gallant, Grant Hill, and I took the right side in order to circle the back. There we found several buildings which we approached cautiously. Down a small lane we heard some excited talking and we immediately investigated. Several children were there and one of them was on the ground. I thought he had been hurt but upon a closer look it proved he was having an epileptic seizure. Roy, who spoke fluent French, questioned the children as to what had happened. They responded in unison saying that the Germans had just been there and had gone down the path. I couldn't leave the boy with the seizure so I bent down to help. He had swallowed his tongue, but with Roy's help I was able to pull it out. I placed a small piece of wood that I found nearby, in the boys mouth between his teeth. This prevented him from biting his tongue. Feeling the boy was alright; we picked up our weapons and pursued the Germans down the path. It was soon obvious that we were too late to catch them, so we returned to the Chateau and found Captain Cook and the rest of the squad.

The Chateau was occupied and the lady of the house invited us in for a meal. This was certainly a strange experience to have happen to you when you are in a foreign land and fighting the enemy. It was like taking a break in reality, or maybe what I was doing was not real. It was hard to imagine that people had to go on living, even though their world was being turned upside down. I wondered, at the time, how I would have reacted had I been in the spot she found herself. Who knows, her husband could have been part of the underground force...maybe the same one we were working with.

CHAPTER III

Things were beginning to jell. German troops began moving out of Eguzon early in the morning. It was now about the 16th of August. At that point no attempt was made to stop them, however, Cpt. Cook with several men, including myself, set out to block the road between Argenton and Eguzon. Trees were felled and one bridge was blown. This was to prevent the Germans from returning in case an attack was planned before they returned. On August 18th, I went out with Capt. Cook and seven other men to set up an ambush. We were told there would be a movement of Germans. We were accompanied by a large number of Maquis. We had chosen our ambush location in a nice secluded area. Plenty of trees were located behind us and the road provided unlimited visibility in both directions. After setting up we sat down to await the arrival of the enemy. We covered an area about one-half mile long. The French Marquis comprised the greater number of the troops. We, being only seven in number, were interspersed along the line of underground fighters. We all carried small weapons. No guns larger than a 30 caliber machine gun were used. This was to be a hit-and-run operation. When the Germans arrived in the line of fire, we would use every available weapon on them and immediately withdraw into the woods and disappear.

The first day passed without activity. We had with us some K-rations and so we were not at the point of being starved. None-the-less, the inactivity of being in one place and waiting for something to happen, tended to work on our nerves. All of this was to end shortly. The next day around noon the local inhabitants found out where we were hiding and came out in number, including women and children. They brought with them large loaves of bread and bottles of wine. I remember one woman in particular pushing a wheelbarrow with a barrel of wine bouncing jauntily along. They also brought with them the information that the Germans had taken another route. What started out to be a fire fight became a welcome party. They were anxious to see the Americans. For some, we were the first and only Americans they had seen. Groups of people like this got to be one of the problems we had to put up with.

We were constantly plagued with informers. The FTP, or French Communists, were informing on us, as well as various citizens that felt the Germans would prevail. It was next to impossible to ferret out all of these people, even though the F.F.I. (French Forces of the Interior) or Maquis were doing the best they could. Because of the loosely knit underground it was always a problem to keep things completely controlled, and so we had to live under the specter of betrayal.

With this ill-fated ambush past and the fact that the Germans were leaving Eguzon, we made our move to take over the city. When we first took possession of the city of Eguzon, the French forces led by Capt. Clavel, placed their heavy weapons squad, together with a heavy mortar, in the camp to strengthen the defenses and to keep the French units under control. Eguzon was a key position to control. It was on the main route of the Germans, as they pulled out of France on their way back to Germany.

On August 20th plans were completed for the defense of Eguzon. Capt. Cook set out with the demolition squad, who with Rudy Dolozal in charge, blew up two bridges near the city of Crozaunt. One of the bridges was a triple span constructed of stone and cement with steel reinforcements. Blowing this bridge was a spectacle that delighted the local population. They knew for sure they would be secure from the return of the Germans.

Having taken the city of Eguzon, Commandant LeClair

of the Maquis, Capt. Clavel of the first French Regiment, and we Americans continued to organize and strengthen the defenses of Eguzon. It was decided that the First French Regiment would continue to hold the near perimeter posts around the transformer, dam, and turbine equipment while the Maquis would hold the two outer perimeters. One was a distance of about a mile and a half, and the other one about a 10 mile radius. This was done to prevent any German troops from coming too close to the vital installations. With all this area to cover, it was found that we did not have sufficient troops. More Maquis were required and so word was put out for additional volunteers. During the next week 600 additional men were added.

During this time of building, contact was established with a Capt. Edward at Freseline, about ten miles to the south of us. He was in charge of the Maquis in and around the Creuze region. He helped enormously in cutting roads in that region south and east of Eguzon. In the west, Capt. Richard organized the cutting of roads in the region of St. Benoit and Pressas. This extended the whole perimeter of defense to about 20 to 25 miles of the installations.

In the meantime, Chateauroux was liberated and the French Maquis staged a parade in celebration on the 28th of August and invited us to take part in the event. The various companies of the Maquis, as well as the Americans, took part in a parade. A wreath was laid at the grave of the Unknown Soldier at Argenton, as well as at Chateuroux, amidst great cheers and acclamation from the crowds. Many speeches were made by the local dignitaries and much expression was given by the women and children.

Before the speeches were finished word arrived that large columns of Germans had moved from Bordeaux, through the city of Chatallerault, west and north of Argenton and were located west of Poiteirs extending to the city of Meziers, supposedly heading northeast. The Germans had moved into Chatallerault and had shot the mayor and several officials. Hearing all of this, we immediately returned to LeBlanc. This was still our base of operation. Soon after arriving, Capt. Cook took me and several other men and set out to reconnoiter the roads leading form Tournon to LeBlanc and Tournon to Lureil. Not seeing any sign of Germans, we had stopped for a moment. At this time four of the men decided to take a short run toward the city of Yzeures. This was just a small town and not very far away. They were in a German jeep. We had decided to return to LeBlanc when the men returned. It looked as if the Germans had continued on, or had taken another route. Well, it didn't take but a few minutes before we saw them reappear in a cloud of dust. They had run smack into a road block of Germans. Their jeep slowed long enough to yell at us to follow because the enemy was "thicker than fleas on a dog". We followed in hot pursuit. Eight of us were no match for the number of Germans they reported seeing. From what we could gather, the Germans would not use the road leading to LeBlanc. It was decided they would use the road between Tournon and Lureil, and so an ambush was planned two miles east of Tournon.

A message arrived for Lt. Col. Oblinski saying that the Germans had given the citizens of Tournon and ultimatum stating that hostages would be shot if the road was not cleared by 9:00 that evening. Oblinski immediately sent a letter to the Germans demanding their surrender, and that we should have their answer within 12 hours. Our demand was delivered to the Germans by a local priest. It was felt this would be safer than sending one of our officers. Whoever we sent would not be allowed to return. Nevertheless, the following day the priest returned saying the Germans would respond with force. We had now committed ourselves. We immediately boarded trucks and sped as fast as possible to the chosen site on the road, about a mile west of Lureil. I could feel the adrenaline speeding into my system. The truck I was in was rumbling along at a speed that made me feel exhilarated. Something was up and I was a part of it.

Almost before we came to a complete stop some of the men were jumping to the ground. It felt good to get some of the men out of the trucks - we were packed in like sardines. It was late in the afternoon, but still light enough to see that the left flank was covered by the Maquis. They had two Bren Guns, one placed on a hill and the other covering the road on which the Germans were expected to approach. Of course interspersed between and around these guns were many of the underground with a variety of weapons -- those supplied by us as well as those taken from the Germans. Capt. Cook took our squad about 150 yards further on to the left of this road. We were equipped with two bazookas and one Bren gun; besides the rifles we all carried. At this point Capt. Cook took me with him and we moved down a slight incline along a hedgerow toward the road. It was as if we were on a Sunday afternoon stroll - talking of various things such as the growth of the brush that formed the hedgerow and remarking at the beauty of the fields that made up the area of ambush. Hedgerows were a common thing in France. They provided boundary lines between farms and provided wind breaks against the elements. It was just a pleasant walk and we were having little to no realization of what would take place within a few short hours.

Lt. Col. Oblinski had taken some men and had covered the right flank. He had with him a Bren gun and several rifles. We had also brought a 3" mortar, and this was placed on the east side of the road to cover the approach of the Germans. Interspersed among us were the Maquis. It was difficult to determine the exact number, as they come from all walks of life and from all directions. As soon as the call went out, the underground responded in force. By the time we came on the scene, many had been there for some time waiting our arrival.

Capt. Cook and I waited. This was always the most difficult part of any ambush. It was approaching 2300 hours, or about eleven o'clock. Suddenly we heard the rumble of trucks and the familiar sound that comes from the movement of troops. At this point a remarkable thing happened. One man came into view riding a bicycle. He must have been the advance scout. It was obvious the Germans planned to sacrifice him to warn them of any resistance. I can see it all yet. The French underground had bazookas supplied by us, and one of them must have thought it would be a good way to start things off. As soon as the shell hit the man on the bicycle, the Germans deployed. The information given to us had led us to believe that we were to encounter a small force of about 100 men. This was far from the truth. What we found out later was that this small German unit was a vanguard of two German divisions. No wonder the answer to our request for them to surrender was ignored!

They drove up in trucks, deployed in perfect formation, and attacked simultaneously from the front and rear trying to destroy our rear line-up. This is where Capt. Cook and I were located with our squad. From our vantage point, Capt., Cook and I were vulnerable. Down the hedgerow that we had walked some three or four hours earlier, we could now see the faces of the enemy. It didn't take long to decide we were in a bad spot. At this time, the Germans had not yet seen us.

"Come on Johnny", yelled the Captain "We're in a bad spot."

"You're telling me?" I yelled back. "You can stay if you want, but I'm leaving."

At that point we both started back up the incline along the hedgerow and back to where the rest of the squad was located. Our return was hastened because the Germans had seen us and they began to fire a 20 mm. cannon after us as we retreated. Casually walking down three or four hours before, now became a run for our lives. Glancing over my shoulder, I could see the shells bursting behind us. I don't know which one of us came in first but we were breathing hard from the run. At about this same time, the Germans came up in great force around Col. Oblinski's right flank, coming to within 15 to 20 yards of the command post. There were a number of our men here, as well as many Maquis. Hand grenades were thrown at the enemy and several were killed, as well as many wounded. This stopped the German flanking movement and they withdrew.

Lt. Dumont, with his squad covering the right flank of the ambush, was in a small clump of woods bordering the road. On his left were small numbers of Maquis extending down to a point which traversed the road. Directly to Lt. Dumont's right was a mortar squad. At a little after 2300 hours Lt. Col. Oblinski's men began firing. Just prior to this, we in Capt. Cooks' squad had already made contact with the enemy and were laying down a barrage of bullets. About 20 minutes after we had opened fire, Lt. Dumont began laying down a mortar barrage, trying to stop the Germans from overrunning our flank. Upon seeing what was happening, Dumont's forward observer quickly returned to the mortar squad and stopped them from firing, because they were operating too close to where we were. We thought the Germans were doing the mortaring, and it wasn't until later that we found out our own men were responsible. It was so dark, and with so much confusion going on, it was not a bit surpassing that something like this could happen.

We were doing the best we could against great odds, and were hoping the call to withdraw would some soon. Compared with the two divisions facing us, we were a small handful of people. We had to remind ourselves we were not here to win the war by ourselves, but merely to harass and delay the Germans on their return to the Fatherland.

Not making it known to Lt. Dumont, the Maquis forces on his left flank withdrew, taking with them two of his men. These two had been guarding the entrance to the woods. The reason they did this, we found out later, was that they were told that Lt. Dumont had been killed along with the rest of his men. During the time that Lt. Dumont was guarding the right flank on top of the road, Capt. Cook and I, along with our squad, were holding the left flank parallel to the road. A hill of considerable size separated the two squads. Our men were placed at about 150 foot intervals with Maquis filling the gaps in between. We were equipped with one bazooka and one Bren gun. The rest of us had rifles. A farm house was located about 100 yards down the road from where we were, and it was discovered shortly after this that the Germans were making a flanking movement behind that farm house. This put us in a bad spot. Cpl. Harnois, our Bren gunner opened fire on them and was able to break up the encirclement. The Germans realized we had positions on this flank and soon withdrew.

It was now completely dark and at this point Capt. Cook and some of the men withdrew to a point about 300 yards to the rear. In the darkness, and with the rain beginning to come down, three of us became separated and lost contact with the main body of the squad. To make it worse, we were not told of the re-assembly point four miles to the south, at a farm house near a small village. Roy Gallant, Tom McQuire, and I walked what seemed like several miles, but was not very far. We could still hear faint sounds of firing. It must be that some of the Maquis had not given up as yet. In walking, we discovered we had crossed the main road the Germans had used when they ran into our ambush. We were now considerably to the left of the area where we made contact with the enemy. Suddenly, out of the gloom a large woods appeared ahead of us. We were miserably wet and tired. Everything looked fairly safe and so we lay down on the soft, wet floor of the woods and it wasn't long before we were asleep. It was now somewhere around 2:00 in the morning. After about three hours sleep I woke up to see a silvery gray light in the east. I shook the other two men and we prepared to leave and try to find the rest of our outfit.

It was a good thing Roy was with us because he spoke French. If it wasn't for him, Tom and I would have had a great time trying to make ourselves understood. We moved out to the road again and found the farmhouse that had been seen on our entry to the woods the night before. This was the same house that Harnois had driven the Germans away from during our firefight. The farmer saw us coming and immediately directed us to the barn. He told us to bury ourselves in the hay and he would get us something to eat. Having had no food since the previous day, this sounded like something we could use and we eagerly awaited his return. When he did return, Roy asked him if he had seen any Germans. He said he had not seen any since yesterday but that we should hide just to make sure.

That same morning Capt. Cook and two men set out looking for us. They had returned to the battle site, thinking that we may have been killed. No Germans were encountered, but they did find an abandoned car. This they took, and as we were just finishing our bread, wine and cheese we heard a vehicle drive up. When we heard this we poked our heads up cautiously and peeked out of the hayloft window. We could hear English words spoken and so we knew someone had come to find us. We surely were happy to see the captain and the men he had with him.

CHAPTER IV

When everyone was finally assembled back to Eguzon a message was waiting for Col. Oblinski that told him he was relieved of his duties there and that he was to move on to another area. Capt. Cook then took over command and we worked with the F.F.I. commanders in the area, a Major Hugh and a Major Franck. From there we went with Major Franck back to LeBlanc, so we could be within striking distance of Eguzon if the need came to ward off any further attack by the Germans. Patrols were sent out, but by this time the long German column had passed.

For the next two days, beginning on the 7th of Sept., Capt. Cook, and seven of us in his squad, reconnoitered the area near a secondary highway leading up to the city of Chatearoux, which the Germans had been using for their retreat. We were informed by a local farmer that the Germans had been bivouacked within a few hundred yards of this highway. We scouted in both directions trying to locate them. The surrounding woods and highway were littered with a lot of equipment belonging to the Germans. I remember going through a wooded area and seeing a mound of dirt, just freshly laid with a German rifle stuck in the ground supported by its bayonet. On the top of the rifle was a German helmet. This must have been a casualty resulting from the battle we had had with them two weeks before.

Our work seemed to be coming to a close in this assignment. Several patrols were conducted around the areas of Eguzon and Chateuroux, but no sign of the enemy showed up. The French were stronger now and were certainly better equipped. With the Germans out of the area, or at least on the run, the local population felt it was necessary to make examples of those women who had fraternized with the

Germans. In the city of Argenton, we saw women taken to the public square to have their heads shaved. This was done to signify to the rest of the people their disgrace for the things they had done to their countrymen.

Plans were now underway to get out, so a small field was chosen that could be reached by a C-47 airplane. We radioed that we would be in a field just north of the city of Chateauroux on the 13th of September. Early that morning we set out to capture this small field. As was often the case, some little pockets of Germans were left behind. This small air field was still being used by the Germans for pilots that had to have their planes re-fueled, and also to have a place for minor repairs. We chose the date well. We never knew if it was by shrewd calculation or just plain luck, but there were no German planes on the field at the time. We only had to hold the field for a short period and we were hoping the rest of the operation would go as well. After encircling the control tower and the barracks, with the help of the underground, we advanced. Surprise was on our side. Before the small German element involved could make a move, we had secured the field and were now awaiting the arrival of our plane. You could see the surprise on the face of the airfield commander. He probably thought he had seen his last days. Whether or not he knew about the Americans in the area, or whether he figured he would be overrun eventually, we will never know. All we wanted to do was use his field for a short time in order to get out. What happened after that was his problem. What the underground did we no longer had any control over since as soon as we left the ground things were out of our hands.

Well, it didn't take long before we heard the drone of the plane's engines, and soon after that the wheels set down on the grassy field. All we took back with us were our weapons, so loading was no problem. As you might expect, there was nothing less than a Major in the group picking us up. It seemed that everyone that wanted a visit to occupied France, looked for the opportunity to get there. The Maquis had brought with them many bottles of champagne. These were opened as a celebration of our leaving them. A jovial mood was in the air by the time we were ready to take off. Down the field we rumbled and became airborne in a state of rollicking laughter. The pilot, in a mood of generosity, give us a bird's-eye view of the bombed areas that the Eighth Air force had given to many of the cities. We had a terrific trip back! The navigator was in no position to tell us where we were. Finally, Capt. Cook took our land map and directed us toward the coast of France. From there we could tell we were heading for the coast of England.

We had to stay under the coastal radar as we were an unscheduled flight. Outside of one small contingent of the Eighth Air force, very few knew of the existence of the O.S.S. so the pilots could not submit a flight plan. If anything would happen, no one would admit to having known about us. We were taking the chance of being an unidentified aircraft, and therefore being an enemy plane. Coming in over the channel, we were between one and two hundred feet off the water. It seemed the waves could be touched by our hands if we could reach out. We were fascinated by the closeness of the water. While in this state of fascination, we sighted the White Cliffs of Dover. As they moved towards us the song written about them came to mind. We soared higher and higher to avoid crashing into them and rode over their tops as gracefully as a gull when approaching an obstacle. Good, we hadn't been detected by English radar and no fighters had intercepted us. As soon as we were over friendly soil, our pilot radioed Harrington Field that we were on the way. Our mission accomplished, we felt we had done the job assigned us and we were ready for whatever came our way next.

CHAPTER V

We arrived back at Brockhall and things sure looked good to me. I had been through quite a bit more than I thought I would ever do in the short time I had been around. I am sure most of the men felt the same way. Could we ever go back to being the same men we were when we first came into the service? This was something that entered my mind as we all gathered in the main hall of the Manor Brockhall for our debriefing.

Our squad tents were still pitched, and we found our old bunks ... the same ones we had occupied before we jumped into France. After our debriefing, we were allowed to go out on short passes. The debriefing consisted of trying to remember all of the things that happened to us during the time we were in France and especially while under fire. Trying to put everything into the proper perspective was not an easy task. We were all glad when this part was finished.

A place we visited often before we jumped into France was a little pub called the "Spotted Cow". It was just down the road from the city of Whedon, and a short distance from Brockhall. We could get there by walking through fields. This was by far the shorter distance. This had become a regular hangout for us prior to our jump, and now we were eager to go back and let our English friends know that we were all right. It was a quiet place and typical of the setting one would expect of an English Pub. The name must have had some significance to the locals, even though it seemed a strange one to us. Darts and cribbage were the evening's entertainment, and a good many times I was beaten by the men who played it on a regular basis. This always cost me a pint of Bitters, but I was happy to pay up ... it made the old boys at the pub feel good.

After our debriefing period, we were also allowed

passes to Northhampton. This was a fairly good sized city about 9 miles from Brockhall. Some of us that had already been debriefed were allowed to go in for the evening. On one occasion several of us hopped the truck for Northhampton, and spent the evening at a movie, and then stopped off at the USO club for a cup of tea and a sweet roll. When the call came that the truck was ready to return, I failed to exit the USO on time and watched as its taillights became smaller and smaller. I was left alone and nine miles from camp. Well, I'd been alone before and I did know the direction back to camp.

I set out on foot, but I knew it would be a long walk! As I left the city of Northhampton, the fog began rolling in. Now England is known for its fogs and this one was as good as they come. It was soon evident that I was not alone. I heard, in the distance, a faint clipping of heels as they beat a tattoo on the black topped highway. As they approached me I imagined all sort of things that could take place. Jack-the-ripper had returned - the hounds of the Baskerville would soon be heard - Sherlock Holmes would soon be approaching. Out of the fog a silhouette was beginning to form. The sounds became louder and suddenly, "Even'n mate. Somewhat of a fog you know?" "Miss your truck?" And with that he was off before I could acknowledge his presence. Interesting people these English.

I knew I had to be back by reveille at 6:00 A.M., but it was around 12:30 when I passed through the gate by the guard house leading to camp. I was plenty damp, because of the fog, but no worse for the 9 mile walk. I would certainly make sure to catch the return truck next time!

After we had settled in for a few days, we were given a seven day leave. We could go anywhere we wanted to. Some of the men went to Ireland, but I chose London. It had always looked good to me. I thought it would be nice to see the city that we had heard so much about. Even the train ride was a novelty. The passenger coaches had doors that opened to the platform. Each door was an entrance to a compartment that would seat 6 people in comfort. We traveled with about twice that amount in each compartment, together with many standing in the hallway that connected each compartment. This caused the conductor to do a lot of pushing and shoving to make his way between compartments to collect tickets. Getting on the train in Northhampton brought us to London in about an hour and a half. Most of the riders on the train were in uniform. I had two months' pay on me and I could live well.

Seeing the city of London was more of a shock than anything. The Germans had done their job well - London was a shambles. Not only had Jerry bombed the city by airplane, but recently had used the V-2 rockets. As a matter of fact the V-2's were still being used while I was there. I suppose these were the beginning of what we now know as missiles. They appeared to be a long tube with fins on the rear to guide them, and when they stopped running and the motor quit, you had to wait just a short time before the explosion could be heard and felt. Just about every building was demolished or in such bad shape that it could not be used, or even identified as a building.

"Here comes one now", someone shouted. It could be heard a good distance away. I ran out of the hotel I was staying in, and because it was night, you could see the flames shooting out of the back of it as it threaded its way to the end of its flight. The engine stopped and you could see the V-2 stop in midair and slowly make its descent to the ground. Each one was provided with a certain amount of fuel that would carry it to various parts of London or the surrounding area. The V-2 was in constant use now, and even when we returned to Brockhall we would occasionally see one go overhead. The city of Coventry was north of us and the Germans were trying to put out the power station there. We were told none of them reached that far. The irony of it all would be to be hit by a V-2 rocket after having been through France and returned safely.

Leaves go too fast! When all of us were back at Brockhall we could feel something in the wind. We knew our tour of duty was not over. We also figured with the movement of the war in Europe that we would not go back there. That left only one place and we figured we would all be heading for the Pacific. This soon became evident when it was announced that we could either volunteer for China or be sent back to the regular army. With the choices given us, everyone volunteered to go and so we readied the camp for departure.

We not only had to make the Manor ready but had also to do something with the mascots. We had a dog and a cat. They blended well with each other, but we were not certain about us. The dog was trained to bark at airplanes when they went overhead. You could see him running across fields, looking up and barking until the plane was out of sight. The cat, on the other hand, was taught to parachute. Several of the men had fashioned a parachute out of items we had around. By dropping him from the roof of Brockhall, he would descend gracefully to the ground with claws extended and with what appeared to be a smile on his face. As soon as the ground was contacted he would take off and hide. His parachute was a give-away and he could always be recovered. He seemed to enjoy it as he never left camp. His name was "Geronimo".

Brockhall had to be put back to its original condition so the owners could take possession again. It had only been loaned to the O.S.S. as a staging camp. The tents we occupied were 8-man squad tents ... these had to come down to be stored. A large center pole held up the structure. It was a difficult thing to get someone inside to drop the pole and get out before the entire tent came crashing down around him. The fastest, and by far the safest method, was to tie a rope to the center pole and the other end to a jeep. In a very short time all of the tents were lying on the ground ready to be rolled up and stored.

Some of the men were exceptional thieves. As with any old manor house in England, the owner had accumulated memorabilia in the form of swords, guns, and war items from all parts of the empire. When we took over the manor all of these items were placed in the attic, with this knowledge came the desire to relieve the owner of his possessions. The fact that items were missing did not turn up until we had docked in New York. Lt. Bates took possession of these items at that time and returned them to the owner without delay. Many years after the war it was discovered that these items never arrived at Brockhall; somewhere in shipment someone must have discovered their value and kept them for themselves.

Around the first week of November we were ready and were shipped off once again, arriving at Liverpool to board a ship for the States.

The ship we were to board was the S. S. Marine Raven, and we were to travel unescorted. We were assured that the German U-boats were no threat, and besides we were told the ship could travel at speeds that would probably outrun any submarines. There was no reason to worry, so we put our lives in the hands of the Merchant Marines and boarded without incident. We were additionally informed the trip back home would take only 5 days. I am sure the captain and crew knew we wanted to get home as quickly as possible, thinking we had served our time overseas and this would be the end of our combat service. We didn't have the nerve to tell anyone that we had all volunteered to go to the Pacific Theatre and jump behind Japanese lines.

Things started out fine, but two days out of Liverpool, we ran smack into a typhoon or gale, whatever you wanted to call it. Whatever it was brought high winds and heavy seas that you couldn't believe. Everyone was asked to stay behind closed doors so as not to be washed overboard. Staying inside a closed ship was not the finest way to travel. For two days we pounded into seas that looked to be 20 to 30 feet high. I, for one, had to see the size of the waves for myself. They really fascinated me! With the proper evasive action I was able to get on deck several times during the blow to see just how bad it was. I couldn't believe my eyes!

The days were boring, so the Merchant Marine provided the troops with movies. These were held in the dining room. In order to see the picture properly, all the windows and doors had to be closed or darkened. With the roll of the ship and the darkness of the room, it didn't take long before most of the people watching the movie became sick. Doors flew open and the occupants left, emptying their stomachs. It was enough to make the strongest sailor woozy.

Well, believe it or not we all survived the trip. It took us seven days to make the crossing. The two extra days were spent in the storm. It was daylight and we were entering the harbor of New York.

"Now hear this", came the announcement over the loudspeaker. "We will be passing the Statue of Liberty. It will be on the port side. Only half of you can stand on the side. If you all do, the ship will capsize". Fortunately I was on the port side and could see the grand lady as we slid past. We had fought for liberty and she had represented it. We were thrilled! We pulled up to the dock and an army band greeted us. We sure felt important as we came down the gang-plank to dry land. The good old (two-and-a-half ton) army trucks were waiting for us and we were spirited away amid the music, shouting of the crowds, and just plain feeling good. On arrival at our camp, we were fed a good meal of steak, potatoes, and all the trimmings, plus apple pie and ice cream. It was great to be home and to be an American!

CHAPTER VI

We were not given any leave in New York City, but were shipped back to good old area F outside of Washington. Things looked the same at Area F, but we were not the same. We had entered the O.S.S. as young men, green in many areas of our lives, and were now returning as men who had gone through some experiences that we hoped we would not have to duplicate. We had lost some of our friends. The Swedish group had left England for a drop into Norway after we had returned to Brockhall. They had all been killed. I had lost a fellow medic that I had trained with and had been in France with. These were difficult things to understand, but we accepted them as normal.

We stayed at the Congressional Country Club for about two weeks, going into Washington just about every night. It was now the first of December, 1944, and we were finally given a 30 day leave so we could visit family, and prepare ourselves for our next assignment in China. Snow had come down in abundance and even in Washington there was plenty of it on the ground. Van Timmeran and I decided to hitchhike back home. This saved us considerable cash and besides the trip could prove interesting. We traveled by truck. Truckers were about the only people that had access to gasoline as goods had to be shipped. I am sure the truck drivers felt they were contributing to the war effort by giving servicemen a lift.

I was beginning to change, and 30 days at home became a long time. All of my friends were in the service. Being at home for that leave was an awkward time, not only for me, but for my family as well. Being in the O.S.S., there was very little I could tell them about what I had done. I suppose it made a wall between us. There was nothing I could do about it. Because Van and I lived fairly close to each other we were able to do some things together. He was married and so it posed somewhat of a problem for him also. It was a very frustrating leave and also a time of great transition for me. I had left home as a boy and had now returned for a leave as a man. The reality of another stretch behind enemy lines faced me, and I was unable to say anything to the people I loved. I am sure father was proud of me, but how could anything be exchanged? -- I was sworn to secrecy.

The leave was finally coming to an end and it was decided we would return a week early. Christmas was not yet here, but we felt that going back early would ease the pain back home. By going back early we were certain we could make it back on time. We were traveling by truck and we were certain we would have no delays. The snow was heavy and the travel through Ohio was bad, as the snow was causing problems. We were stuck a few times which caused a few delays. None-the-less, we did arrive with only a day to spare. Finally Roy, Jim, Bob, Hob, Grant, Doolie, and all the rest arrived and we were ready for our next assignment. It seemed we were a group destined to be on the move.

While waiting for our orders to move, we visited the little bar, not far from Area F, called Cabin John. It was a place we went to often. It was near the camp and was a place we could meet and go over thing we would do when we got back from this war. We were full of life and had a reckless attitude about everything. We felt that very little could stop us. No matter what we planned in life we would be able to accomplish it. Pitfalls seemed small ditches we could hurdle without effort. Mountains seemed small mounds easily overcome. It was obvious we were still at a point where we were naive. That we understood so little was to be expected as we were young and pliable. The days dragged by and finally we received notice that we were to pack up and move out. We were booked on a fast train out of Washington, and on our way to the west coast. We arrived at Grand Central Station in Washington and entered the doors of this magnificent place. It was so large and had an air about it that made you feel important. The high ceiling and pillared supports made you think you had entered one of the movies seen as a child back home. We moved through the great cavernous halls, carrying our duffel bags, and were escorted through gates to a waiting train.

After arriving in Chicago, we were transferred to the Silver Streak, a fast luxurious train that brought us to Denver, Colorado. From there we were transferred to a train that took us the rest of the way to Los Angeles. What a contrast! The train we were now on was something out of the Wild West days. We crossed and went around the Rocky Mountains, as the case required, and in order to keep warm, small coal burning stoves were at each end that provided very little heat. The seats were also something that defied description. They were little more than wooden benches. Camp Pendleton was our destination and we were very happy to get there. This would end the torture we experienced in travel. We spent 30 days there in our preparation for our exit to the South Pacific.

Hot dog! I could spend a good amount of time in the city of Los Angeles. I thought for sure I would see a lot of movie stars. I may even go visit some of the U.S.O. clubs that everyone spoke of. This was good dreaming because the command there sure had another idea of what we were going to do. Our time was spent in physical training. We did not walk or march to any place on the base. We ran and we ran. It got to be something that we were noted for. Our outfit, being about 50 in number, stood out like a neon light. We ran everywhere and at the same time called cadence so that we were in step all the time. We had excellent military discipline. It wasn't long before the other outfits picked up the idea and were also running instead of walking. Of course, this did not make us too popular with the rest of the camp. Not everyone appreciated our dedication.

It was soon discovered that few had ever seen paratroops on the West Coast. The South Pacific was an area that did not use this type of fighting personnel. The way we wore our pant, bloused over our boots, led many to believe we were pansies. A number of incidents came to a head when our men ran into men from other branches of the service, in town, and had head to head run-ins with them. Everyone in camp soon learned that we were everything we said we were. It wasn't long before things got back to normal and we were viewed in the proper light.

The days went by and it was soon announced that we would board a train and head for San Diego. Here our movements were expedient and we were deposited at the docks ready to board a ship. It wasn't long ago that I had boarded a ship in Newport News, Va. heading for Africa, and now the same thing was happening to me in San Diego. I felt I was spending as much time on the water as I was on land. Maybe I was really a sailor and didn't know it. The bunch of us must really be without common sense. Volunteering for the Pacific theater? After all, how many G.I.'s would willingly go into two wars. We had lucked out in France. Supposing that everything turned out bad over here. I wondered if I had said the proper good-byes. Probably not. How can a young man with the promise of adventure and a good fight expect to feel the reluctance of family and friends to let him go? Ahead was where the excitement was. Seeing the possible disaster was not even anticipated.

The ship we were to enter was a beauty! It was a converted cruise ship, renamed the S.S. General W.A. Mann, which still had the appearance of luxury. I learned that it carried 5,000 men. Wow! All those troops and we were not to have an escort! Here again we were told that we could outrun any enemy ship that we might encounter. If I remember correctly, we were told the very same thing every time we go on board a ship. I wondered sometimes if they really didn't care.

A band was there to see us off, and as they played some stirring martial music, we were escorted aboard and we found our assigned spot below the water line. A daily routine took over. We were awakened at 6:00 A.M. and prepared for breakfast. The size of the ship and the number of men on it meant that we were fed only two meals a day. It took most of the day to feed everyone. The ship's cook kept up a constant meal pattern. Our group was fed about 7:00 A.M. and then again about three in the afternoon. Several hours in between were spent in calisthenics and activities to keep us in shape. Showering and shaving and other personal duties were done in between time. To fill in free time we could go to the ship's library and get books, or go to the movies that were being shown. Most of the movies we had seen several times before on other troops ships, but we watched them anyway. There was always a card game going on during this time and several dollars changed hands. We really had it made! We were the only outfit that had seen combat duty, and because of this we were not required to serve in the kitchen. Naturally, we assisted every time the kitchen help came to get supplies. Our bunks were located right next to the hold that stored the canned goods. In the process of passing the supplies to the mess sergeant, we would divert cases of spam, Vienna sausages, and fruit cocktail. These were hidden under our bunks to be consumed later. With only two meals a day, it was nice to have a midnight snack. We knew we could not get one in the kitchen. After all, we were taught to live off the fat of the land.

The ship used a zigzag pattern in sailing and it wasn't long before we came to the area of the equator. In crossing the equator, there is a ritual that is followed for those that have never done this before. It is an old nautical custom. Before the official ritual, everyone is considered to be a "Pollywog". After the ceremony, everyone becomes a "Shellback". This ritual requires that everyone crawl, on hand and knees, through an open-topped tube of quite some distance. This tube was watched over by the ship's crew. They, of course, were all Shellbacks. Whenever, and at each crew member's discretion, any head appearing above the tube would be flogged by the Shellbacks, using a pillow or some other soft instrument. To say the least, the force of the flogging would send you to the deck. If you managed to crawl the entire length of the tube without being hit, when you emerged from the end of it, you were hit by a spray of water from the ship's fire hose. This was always unexpected and you came out gasping for air. Lying exhausted and wet of the deck we were told that we were now Shellbacks and were issued a diploma to prove it. At least we knew we would not have to go through that ritual again!

Zigzag we did - going far to the north and far to the south until finally one morning we sighted land. We had arrived off the coast of Australia. After all this time we had the opportunity to see dry land. This is all we did too, just look at it. We were anchored in the harbor of Melbourne, just long enough to take on food and fuel. The next morning we were under way again. The next time we would see land was when we arrived in India.

The trip from Australia to India is quite a distance, especially since it was necessary to travel alone and in waters that were not completely clear of enemy subs. As you might know it was necessary, at one point in our trip, to re-fuel. This was an interesting experience. When we were getting low on fuel, a tanker was called out from one of the islands and they met us on the high seas. We were not told from which island they came, but early one morning we were met by a dirty looking vessel that was to give us fuel enough to reach our destination. Both ships pulled alongside each other and lines were shot from one to the other across the waves. We were riding the swells together and a heavy hose was pulled over. This fed us the necessary oil to replenish our empty tanks. Entertainment was limited on the ship, and as we had seen the films that we had on board several times, we were ready for a change. The tanker had several films they had seen over and over again, so we made an exchange. It was almost like an exchange of books in a library, only we shouted our request across several hundred feet of water. After deciding on the ones we wanted, the films were placed in a bag and with the use of one of the lines that fed us the fuel hose, we received new films. This was accomplished with loud shouts of praise and hoots of welcome from both sides. Having been confined aboard ship for such a long time, little things like the two ships meeting on the open water became a monumental experience.

Chapter VII

Boat traffic became evident. Some were Navy ships in the process of entering the harbor or leaving for extended duty. Others were like ours, ships laden with cargo for military use. Many of them were of a local nature - independent owners, either carrying a form of cargo or people to be deposited at stops along their way to many destinations. Some were fishing boats, intent on providing food for the local population. In the distance you could see land rising from the water. We felt good. We were sick of boat life and travel on the high seas. A cruise ship we were not. Through all the boat traffic we could see one in particular heading our way. It didn't take long before we were boarded and a harbor pilot came on deck to take us into Bombay harbor. Thirty days had passed since leaving San Diego and we were happy to be at the end of our trip. It seemed I was putting as much time on the water as some sailors. Maybe I was really in the Navy and didn't know it.

We stayed on board the ship that night, tied to the dock. The army moves at its own pace. I always had difficulty appreciating the pace at which things were done. Waiting became the normal thing to do. Whenever an order was given, we were expected to obey. Our training always taught us to give an immediate response to orders, but we also knew that we would have to spend time waiting to allow the execution of the orders to catch up with the command.

Anyway, the next morning right after a good breakfast, we were marched down the gangplank and into waiting trucks. The O.S.S. had a way of being there when needed. Our outfit was the only one that got off that morning. The army was slower than we were. We knew we had to get to China, but we were to discover that it would take a long time to accomplish that. Many routes, many methods, and many days would separate us from our final destination.

The trucks finally brought us to the train station and we were placed in regular passenger cars. Unlike the ones in North Africa, these had real honest seats and toilets at one end, just like back in the States. The English, having been in India many years, had westernized many comforts and we were happy to take part in this.

Ah! What luxury! Comfortable seats to sit on, and they would even serve as beds when we became too exhausted to do anything else but sleep. It seemed our outfit was destined to be put into situations that were inconvenient and cramped and generally relegated to places that were out of the ordinary and not what we would expect. We lived our lives on the edge of everything and so this was nothing to be concerned about.

The trip would take us five days to cross over to Calcutta. The people were so poor, and there were plenty of them. We watched them at every stop.

"Don't allow the locals to board our train", spoke our Captain. "These people will take anything and everything they can get their hands on."

When the train stopped, a guard was posted at each end of the car. This did not stop the locals from offering us every type of fruit, vegetable and assortment of artifacts that were made by the local artisans. Gems and stones of all sorts were available. I didn't buy any because I was not sure whether they were the real thing, or just cut glass. After all, we were not the first Americans to travel the width of India, and I am certain these people sold the good stuff to the first troops to come along.

Beggars were in abundance and little children, in tattered clothes or naked, asked for a few handouts. We had been issued a goodly ration of chocolate and cookies when we started the trip, but they did not last long. The children tugged at our heartstrings and so we gave generously, until we ran out. As soon as we were offering something on one side of the train, another unfortunate child on the other side climbed up trying to reach in a window to steal whatever he could touch. It didn't take long before we developed a hard attitude toward the beggars.

Many times, as we ghosted through the towns, we could see the women washing garments at a stream of water. Occasionally a pump or artesian well would come into view. This was used by the population for bathing, drinking and washing. Sometimes all three at the same time.

The days became routine. Villages, towns and cities all looked alike. There certainly was a contrast between India and the United States. In India people were everywhere. It didn't appear that much of the country was unpopulated. I suppose that is what made the country and the people so poor ... there were so many of them.

All of us traveling this route had difficulty accepting the fact that the Brahma bull was seen everywhere. He invaded homes, bazaar stalls, and everything that seemed to take his fancy. It would seem to be good source of food. But we had to understand that this was the Sacred Cow of India. This was the re-incarnation of friends and relatives. Who, in their right mind, would devour their sister, brother, father or mother.

The five days on the train seemed forever, but finally we came into the station in the ancient city of Calcutta. This held much mystique. It was larger than Bombay, but unfortunately it would be almost a year before I would be able to spend any time in it. The famous Bazaar in Calcutta was one place I did not want to miss. It would have to wait though, as we had a mission to perform first. This mission was to formulate, train, and equip a detachment of 20 Chinese Commando Units that could work behind the Japanese lines.

Meetings had already taken place in January of 1945, just two months before our arrival, between Col. Cox, of the O.S.S., General Wedemeyer and General Chaing-Kai-Shek. These three agreed that well trained Chinese, with the help of combat veteran Americans, could work effectively behind Japanese lines to extract intelligence and thwart the work of the enemy. It was interesting to learn that the army high command kept fighting us, thinking that the regular army troops could do this job. We were specialized in this field and had the know-how to carry it off.

Here again we were shuttled off by truck. A day's drive ended in the city of Agra, home of the Taj-Mahal, and at Camp Kanchupara, where many outfits were waiting assignment as replacements to other army units. Being O.S.S. and nobody knowing about us, we had to travel as detached enlisted men. This made us vulnerable to being drafted by any army unit that needed a replacement.

We all piled out of the trucks. I had on the usual back pack, M-1 rifle with cartridges, and a side arm. As I landed on the ground I felt my back snap. All the jumps I had made, all the physical training I had endured, all the exercises I had gone through to this point, and now my back gives out on me. I hobbled into the barracks, chose a cot, and dumped everything on it. Boy was I angry! Everyone was ready to help though, and so I took charge. I had my two medical kits with me and in these were some 2" wide adhesive tape. I removed my shirt and tore off two pieces of tape about two feet long. With the help of Rudy Dolozal and Roy Gallant I was able to ease the strain on my back muscles. The tape acted as an additional muscle support. It worked fine but it did take a long time for me to heal. The pain is still with me after all these years. I suppose the logical thing would have been to report to sick call, but by doing this I would have been left behind when our outfit finally moved out. After coming this far I was not about to leave my friends.

Every time a request came through for a specialized replacement, Captain Cook had to literally fight headquarters to retain our outfit intact. Radio operators and medics were especially needed, and so were in great demand. To get out of there was vital, and to do so as soon as possible.

To get to Kunming became a challenge for us. We had to cross the "Hump". This referred to the Himalayan Mountain range that separated China from India, and was located in the country of Burma. The trip over and back was made daily by C-47 airplanes. Dozens of them were used to fly equipment and men back and forth. To get a seat on one of these required a pass. A pass was issued only to those that qualified. To qualify you had to be important or have an important mission. We had an important mission all right, but as we had only a Captain as our leader, and we were traveling as detached enlisted men, it put us way down the list as qualified. We had about as much chance to fly as it did to see snow in New Delhi.

We spent cautious days in camp dodging replacement attempts, while Captain Cook tried every angle to get us out of there. Finally word came that the British had a convoy of trucks and jeeps going to Kunming. They needed drives and would we like the job. It didn't take long before we were all packed and ready to go.

I was assigned a jeep. Perfect. I was sure exited. The only driving I had done prior to that was in my father's old model A Ford. I had not driven since I was in the army, except to receive my license when I was back home for my 30 day leave. The police at home were very generous in giving out licenses to servicemen. I did not take an exam, but I did drive around the block. The driving exam was short because gas was rationed, so the police were generous. Now was my golden opportunity to apply my talents as a driver.

We were off and running. Our column left around the 3rd of April 1945, and it would take us until the 15th of April to arrive in Kunming. We tried to average 100 miles a day. The afternoon of the day we left brought us very near the Taj-Mahal, in the city of Agra. I could see it on my left as I was driving along, standing majestically in the open, its gold dome reflecting the sun's rays. I guess everyone had heard of the Taj-Mahal but none of us had ever seen it. The movies did not do it justice. It was massive. It was well fenced and secured, but we were on the road and could do little more than look as we sped past.

Leaving Calcutta took us over the Bramaputra River to the Ledo Road. The Ledo Road led us from Agra about 400 miles from where we would actually enter the Burma Road. This was at the city of Lashio on the Burma border, then into newly recaptured Burma. Going over the Burma Road we had to cross the Chindwin, Iriwaddy, Salween and Mekong Rivers.

The days on the Burma Road were hot. The road went through and around mountains, and we followed each other like a line of ants looking for a picnic to attack. The climate was tropical, and we followed the road that had been used from ancient times. Travel had to be cautious because the Japanese had not been driven out very many months before. There was always the possibility that there could be some straggling units left in the area. We traveled with our weapons ready, just in case.

The Burma Road had been literally hacked and chewed out of the Himalayan Mountains. The Chinese and Burmese, who built the road, had no modern equipment. They would chisel and blast with black powder, removing the stones and gravel by hand. Hundreds and thousands of them worked back-breaking hours to accomplish this feat. Many times, during our stay in China, I would witness this very thing. The road was just wide enough in spots to allow the passing of two trucks, but in other places, especially on curves, room for one truck is all that you could expect. At these times it was a matter of who would bluff the other into stopping or pulling off to let one of them pass.

Some areas we drove through were very picturesque, but we saw no towns or villages. They must have been located in the hills and wooded areas. Occasionally we would see a Burmese family or individual as we drove past. I am sure they kept to themselves. On one occasion we took a lunch break along the road near a spot that was blanketed with orchids. By the time I left there my jeep was well decorated with them. The only bad part was that the orchids did not last long after picking.

Sleeping at night in a tropical zone proved to be a challenge. Mosquitoes and biting bugs ruled the night. To survive, we slept on the roofs of the trucks. This got us up far enough to minimize the fight against the stinging, so we could get some badly needed rest.

Our travel took us to a place on the road that I'll never forget. We had left Leingling and were now beginning to ascend mountains where the road virtually clung to its side. It was a steady climb upwards. Hairpin turns were traversed and looking back I could see the trucks appearing and disappearing behind outcroppings. The next stop we were heading for was called Paoshan, China. It was 60 miles by crow flight, but about 125 to 150 miles by road. The view from the top of the mountain we just crested was spectacular. We could not stop to take in the view and so had to push on. I could see the road now take a steep downgrade. It was necessary to put the jeep into a lower gear and creep down without plummeting off the side. Finally we arrived in the foothills of this mountain and saw before us the Salween River. Straight before us was a high ravine. We crept slower along the road, and to the left of us was the edge of a drop going down several hundred feet.

59

We stopped. Just ahead was a bridge. I said to Jim Gardner, our radio man, "They expect us to go over that?" He responded by saying he doubted we could fly over. It was judged to be several hundred feet long and swayed in the breeze that constantly moved through the ravine. When we first arrived we could not tell what the cables, that suspended the bridge, were made of. It must have been used by the Burmese and Chinese for years. It appeared to have vines and bamboo woven together. It was soon discovered that the Japanese had strengthened the bridge by using steel cable. Outside of driving around the mountain, and that was impossible, it constituted the only means of crossing. The local people assured us that the Japanese had sent tanks and trucks over regularly when they occupied the country. We had few options at this point.

Looking down we could see the Salween River raging below as it cascaded between the rocks. The Salween River Bridge looked weak, and I was certain it would collapse the minute we used it. A group of Burmese were on hand to assist us in the crossing. They were all smiles - bobbing and swaying in good oriental custom. It was also pointed out that only one vehicle at a time could use the bridge.

This made me feel better. Boy, could we get ourselves into something! As each vehicle would enter the suspension, it would sag. The trucks and jeeps appeared as though they were going through a tube, something like stuffing sausage. It took us all of that day to cross, and it was done without difficulty. Finally, when all of the vehicles had arrived on the other side, we drove a few miles further on and camped for the night. We had found an area along the side of the Salween River that provided us with enough parking space to accommodate the entire convoy.

We had been issued a good supply of army rations, but when possible we would stop at an army camp or outpost to get a good hot meal and a shower. Believe me, it was not very often. The only camps we found were manned by Army engineers who maintained the road. Otherwise sleeping and eating were up to us.

We were finally getting near our destination. The hills and curves were getting monotonous, but we had acquired some skill in driving the road. We had scheduled the trip to make 100 miles a day. After all, it was 1200 miles from Calcutta to Kunming and we figured 12 days was long enough on rations and stale water.

One of our men unfortunately had developed a severe pain in his side. He was running a fever and was nauseous as well. After examining him I determined that he had appendicitis. What to do! We had a Burmese interpreter with us, so I asked him if and where the nearest hospital was located. I was told the Chinese had provisioned a hospital up one of the side roads. This was known as the Bhamo Hospital. We could take him there. It was maybe 10 miles into the mountains to the west of us. They assured me it was staffed by some American and British missionary doctors. It was a good place they said, and they would be happy to show me. I discussed the situation with Capt. Cook and we loaded the patient aboard my jeep. Capt. Cook provided four more men to go along with me in another jeep just in case we ran into some unfriendly forces. It was a wild ride! The man was ill and the road was rough. It was pockmarked from disuse, and rock strewn from the constant erosion of the mountain. We had to make time, but the man was so ill I wanted to make his trip as easy as possible. We had to get to the Bhamo Hospital and back in order to catch up with the main body again. They couldn't afford the luxury of waiting for us. We found the hospital without incident and after checking in with the missionaries, we returned as fast as possible. I don't know what happened to the poor fellow. We never did hear from him again. I suppose he was sent with the first army unit that came along. The rest of the trip consisted of driving the 100 miles a day. We finally arrived in Kunming no worse for the wear. The motor pool as waiting for our arrival and so we deposited the vehicles with the supply Sergeant and reported to headquarters.

Many months prior to our arrival, the Chinese Government had been preparing for us. A small town just north of Kunming about 10 miles, had a place set aside just for our use. It consisted of several buildings on three levels of ground. The buildings were made of clay brick walls and straw thatched roofs. We were motored out there by truck within hours of our arrival. Just before entering the camp, we made a sharp left, and went a short distance, coming to a stop on a flat surface surrounded by high cliffs. We did not stay here. This is where the officers were billeted. They got out of the trucks and the rest of us proceeded another quarter mile further up the hill. We took another sharp left and ran down a slight incline to the parade area. As I was walking up the incline, on my right was a building that would house the clinic and dental office. I was impressed. I knew I would spend some time there. Going a little further I came to the kitchen and mess hall and just beyond that were the barracks. We all headed for this ready to deposit our load and look around. It was quite impressive. A small creek ran through the edge of the parade ground, with a sheer cliff skirting the far edge and extending the full length of the camp. The road we had come from continued on to the west and went out of sight.

CHAPTER VIII

Our assignment in China was completely different from that in France. In France we jumped into an existing underground network that was already functioning. What we became was the catalyst, providing the means and the technique to make it operate effectively and gathering the intelligence necessary to help the Allied invasion forces. In China we had to start from square one to recruit, train and operate an underground espionage group to function behind enemy lines. Because of the nature of the oriental people, we could only be considered advisors. This put us at a distinct disadvantage, in that any work we did would have to be approved by the Chinese Government. Chaing Kai-shek wanted all the glory and credit for everything that went on. We, on the other hand, were wanted and needed, because we provided the intelligence and material necessary to shape the troops and provide the fighting forces.

A commando unit consisted of 181 men. This amounted to 154 Chinese personnel and 19 Americans and eight interpreters. Of the 19 Americans in the unit, two were furnished by S.I. (Secret Intelligence) a division of the O.S.S. These two; one officer and one radio operator, would precede us into the field to prepare for our infiltration.

Our first responsibility was to recruit troops. Because of the nature of the operation, we insisted on having above average men. They had to be the largest ones we could find, as the average was small. They had to have average intelligence, or above average, as we had a lot of technical information to get across. I think we nearly failed in both fields, but we took the best of the recruits we could find. Of the 20 units originally requested, we needed five commando units right away. Needless to say, a goodly number were interviewed before we came up with enough. These five were the only ones that ever materialized and were made ready for the field.

The Chinese officers that were already chosen had been hand-picked by Chiang Kai-shek to fill his purposes. We found out later, after the war had ended, that many of the officers and men were Communists. Before we left China we were to see a different side of these troops.

Nevertheless, we had our troops assigned to us and we began to train them. One of the first people I was introduced to was my interpreter. He was a medical student and was to be my personal interpreter for the duration of the conflict. We became very close friends. His name was Chang Chin Yin. Through him I would bring to the troops all of the shots and medical necessities required to make them healthy. This became my first item of concern; their physical health. All of the troops were given a good going over by Dr. Hamlin, who was assigned to our command unit. He did not jump with us however; this was my responsibility when we went into the field.

After checking the Chinese, we found that good food and exercise would go a long way to improving their health. Instead of the usual one meal a day they lived on, we fed them three meals. Included in their diet were vitamins and meat. After their diets were corrected, we went after their teeth.

I was asked to assist here and found to my great dismay that these poor people needed a lot of work. Tooth extraction was one of the first priorities. These were the easy ones. A little Novocain and out the tooth would pop. I found by working with these people that they would complain and carry on about little things like tooth work, but would not say much, or show little pain, when they were hit by a bullet. This I thought was a marvel. In some cases, when working on the

Chinese, we had to hold the patient down in the chair. Drilling and filling teeth was my greatest challenge. All of my training, back in the States, was done with the latest equipment. Here, we were using equipment that operated without electrical power. Our foot became the power plant, and that was not the most reliable. Believe me, our feet and legs became mighty tired when they had to be continually pumping at a rapid speed. Occasionally you would slow down from sheer exhaustion. This posed a problem for the doctor because the drill would slow down. Everyone became edgy at those times and I would have to double my effort in order to complete the ordeal. I was always happy to know that none of my buddies required the services of this equipment.

After getting our commandos in good condition, we proceeded to their training in the use of arms and weapons. Our first objective was to provide a firing range. The best place we could find was just about a mile north of us, up a fairly good sized hill and in a cemetery. Most of the land was put into the production of rice and other necessary crops to sustain the population. To take an area like this for a rifle range would have deprived the populace of needed ground. So the only other area of any size was the local cemetery. After procuring an O.K. from the local magistrate, and paying the usual fee, we persuaded the Chinese to dig a trench. While this was going on, several of us volunteered to unpack and de-grease the 1903 Springfield rifles that were to be used by them. This was the army issued gun during the First World War, and I believe it was packed at that time and had not been looked at until now. We detail-stripped the guns and, with the use of many gallons of gasoline, were able to clean each part and finally re-assemble them again. After doing about two hundred of them in the period of about a week, we were proud of the results and sick of the work involved. Fortunately, each command group cleaned rifles for their own men.

Getting the Chinese to fire the '03 was interesting. Their arms were not long enough for them to hold the rifles properly. This was one of the reasons we wanted the largest men that were available. When the gun was discharged, the kick was so strong that the Chinese would be knocked down, or he would be left with a bruise on his shoulder or arm, depending where he was holding the butt of the gun. We all had a good many laughs over this, but we did the best we could under the circumstances. Time was short and we still had to teach them to parachute. The days went by fast. With so much to do and so little time to do it in, we worked long hours.

Training them to use a compass always seemed an exercise in futility. When a group of them went out, invariably a scouting party had to be sent to find them. We hoped they would never have to use a compass in the field. I could see us looking for and losing half of our men.

We simulated taking a village. We used one of the many small ones nearby. This always brought out the villagers in force, with the mayor and village rulers questioning our purpose. All we could do was ignore them and proceed to "capture" the village, working our way from house to house looking for the "enemy".

The final step arrived when we introduced our commandos to the parachute. Even though we had the pick of the Chinese soldiers, they were a bit short. This posed a problem when it came to fitting them in a harness. All of the straps were made to fit Americans. In spite of this, we shortened the straps a much as possible, but they still did not fit properly. We would have hated to see one of them fall out in midair.

The usual preparations took place - running, push-ups and calisthenics in general. We had to toughen them up. We did not have an old body of a C-47 plane, as we did back in the States, to use for practice, so we constructed a platform which provided a simulated exit door. This allowed the Chinese to get the feel of the exit and it was just high enough to provide the proper impact when they touched the ground. From this structure we taught them to jump and learn to properly "roll" when hitting the ground. You had to throw your right leg out of the door, assume a crouched position, hold the reserve chute with both hands in front, and count 1000 - 1, 1000 - 2, 1000 - 3. At this point the chute should open. At this point we told them that if the chute did not open, they could go back and get a new one. None of them thought this was funny. After repeating the drill many times, we felt they were ready to put into practice all of their training.

At this point we all piled into trucks to make the trip to an airfield outside of Kunming. The C-47's were waiting. Four jumps were required for the Chinese to receive their wings, and they all seemed eager to get going. With the commandos in place and the jump instructor in charge, the planes took off.

There were 17 Americans in our 2nd. Commando Battalion; five officers and 12 enlisted men. We all went out to the drop zone. It was our job to see that the Chinese descended properly, and to assist them where we could as they reached to ground. It became a comic affair. One incident in particular was notorious. When the door of the C-47 is removed for jumping, the hinges are taped so that nothing can get caught in the openings. One of the Chinese was able to dispel this theory. As he came out, the wind blew him against the hinged side and he caught one of the buckles in a small crack. There he hung in a crouched position waiting for the chute to open. He could go no further and the jump master was unable to release him. While the plane was circling the field, a frantic attempt was made to pry him loose. We, on the ground, saw the jump master give a final yank allowing him to float down. All in a day's work, I guess. It only pointed out the problems we encountered. These problems, we discovered, would be with us in one form of another until the war ended.

We received a lot of laughs out of the training program, but finally we were able to press all of the information and instructions into their heads. Graduation was now upon us and we assembled them before us and presented them with wings. These were not the American jump wings, but one designed by the Chinese. Not only did the Chinese receive them, but we Americans were also given Chinese jump wings. We had worked hard and now we were ready to work together as a team.

After graduation everyone was given a short leave. Trucks were made available and many of us wanted to go to Kunming for a little relaxation. Just before we were ready to go, several of our men had already gotten into the two and a half ton truck that would take us to town. This was the usual transportation when going on leave. Among the men waiting in the truck was a fellow named Renee Semard. He had been with us in France and was a person who enjoyed fun. He was always ready to yell a comment when anyone came near. Tricks were a common practice, especially in the barracks. This was to be a time when a trick was inevitable. Rudy Dolozal was also one to enjoy playing a trick. This combination came together in a deadly way this day. With Renee yelling a few choice words and Rudy responding, the results were bad.

The trick about to be played had already been tried when we jumped into France. Along with me and the rest of the men in our B-24 on our way to France, was a fellow named DuBois. Prior to boarding the B-24 he had removed all of the powder from a hand grenade. This left only the firing pin and cap. Now, when you pull the pin on the grenade, all you get is about 5 seconds of "Pssst"! Nothing more. The cap is all that is left with about as much fire power as a Ladyfinger

Firecracker. After we had all exited the plane DuBois pulled the pin, being the last one out, and threw the grenade to the end of the plane. When we returned to England, we found the crew of the bomber and were told of the fright and confusion they went through after our exit. Granted, this was not a wise thing to do, but youth is not always wise. This same act was to take place this fateful day. Evidently Rudy Dolozal had removed all the gun powder from a hand grenade, leaving the firing pin and cap in operation. This time the whole thing went wrong. The grenade fizzed, the firing pin and cap came off, but for some unexplained reason, enough powder must have been left in the base that it caused the cap to explode and parts of it entered Renee's neck and throat.

Two of the men, on the truck, lowered Renee to the ground and carried him over to the medical center. I happened to be there with Dr. Hamlin and we laid him down on the ground. Renee was bleeding badly from a severed artery and the blood was entering his lungs. He was choking in his own blood. Dr. Hamlin removed his fountain pen from his pocket, took out the insides and attempted to run the empty shaft down through the slit he had cut in Renee's wind pipe to get air into his lungs. Everything was happening so fast, and before we could make any improvement Renee passed away. He drowned in his own blood. It seemed strange - going through one enemy operation in France only to be killed in a non-combat situation. It points out the folly of horse play with weapons of destruction. Rudy was completely devastated by this and wandered off by himself to the barracks. I knew he would suffer shock over this and so I followed him; He lay on his bunk with wild glassy eyes. I had taken some morphine with me and gave him a shot. After covering him up I left him to sleep. Things like this happen, but you have to pick up and keep going. Rudy had to accept this because we needed him for the jump we were about to make. Everyone expressed their confidence in him and assured him that what had happened was not to be held against him in any way.

Orders had come through to prepare for our assignment, but it was felt that a couple of days in Kunming would be beneficial to all the troops. I went in with Jim Gardner and David Boak. We soon found out that the social and cultural differences made for dull living. People were everywhere. The buildings were several stories high and families could be seen at every window. It was strictly tenement living. Garbage was everywhere, also, and people dumped everything from the windows. Children were seen in large numbers and they relieved themselves in the gutters and streets. It was so bad that I was happy to get back to the compound where at least we had some idea of sanitation.

CHAPTER IX

The day was July 27th, 1945, and all of our gear, as well as the Chinese Commandos, including ourselves, were driven out to the airfield and packed into eight C-47 airplanes. As we sat there waiting for our departure I could not help but wonder what I had gotten into again. I kept telling myself we had trained these Chinese as best we could. We had provided them with arms and food, and put all we could into making them a viable force. Nevertheless, as I surveyed the 30 some men around me, I could not help but feel that any fighting we might get into would be done in large part by the Americans.

The plane seemed to labor as we took off early that morning. We were headed for a spot about 600 miles from Kunming, deep behind enemy lines. We were about 5000 to 6000 feet high. We had to stay up far enough so that if there was any ground fire, it would not be effective. Boy was it cold! The door of the plane was removed, as is the usual case, so we could jump out. There was no heat in the plane and the cold came through the open door. Fortunately, there was a stack of army blankets in the rear. I wrapped one around me as best I could. With all the gear and equipment we had to carry, it provided little protection.

It is also good to note here that each American had an additional 60 pound bag strapped to his leg. This provided us with additional supplies of ammo and weapons. A pin would release this bag just before we touched the ground. Trying to stay comfortable and warm with this became a challenge.

I am sure everyone was as miserable as I was. We were soon to find out how fast temperature changes can affect you. Six hundred miles later we were to arrive at a point on the map named Li Tze Sin. This was the place we were to drop into. It was a small town with a large Buddha Temple. The temple was to be our bivouac area and home base of operations.

Even though the Buddha temple was located at Li Tze Sin, the largest town nearby was Hung Le Mao. This was about 50 miles east of Hengyeng in Hunan Province, in the middle of the important Japanese supply triangle of Paoching, Hengyeng and Changsha. This is the place where we would be operating. Several important roads - the Hunan-Kwangsi Railroad - the Canton-Hankow Railroad - the Shipping - Teehlu Railroad - as well as the Siang Kiang River met in this area. A spot was located about two or three miles from the temple, where the rice paddies had gone dry. We began descending from a height of 6000 feet to a height of 1000 feet, this being the normal height to jump from. What happened to the temperature was unbelievable. From freezing cold to humid heat gave us the impression we had entered a furnace. The heat rolled in through the open door of the plane and we began shedding all the blankets we had wrapped ourselves in on the way over. The order came to "Stand up and hook up" and we all responded as best we could, considering the distance we had traveled and the equipment we were carrying. Nevertheless, out we went. One of the officers, a Lt. Wm. Albright, lost his helmet while exiting the plane. When the chute came out, a buckle inflicted a good sized gash in his skull. I went right out after him and was able to see what had happened. As soon as we both hit the ground, I patched him up and we arranged our gear for the walk to the Buddha Temple. The helmet was found by one of the Chinese, but he was in no position to wear it.

When I was in training I thought I was in pretty good shape...able to take everything that was directed my way and able to run five miles each day, with or without a pack on my back. I was also able to do calisthenics, able to hold up under pretty strenuous training, able to conserve my energy and tough my way through most anything. I found that nothing had prepared me for what happened next. The heat and humidity on the ground was so heavy that I suffered from heat exhaustion. As a matter of fact, all of the Americans had the same problem. It was so bad that I could not walk without great effort. The first few hundred yards were fairly good, but as I went along I began to walk slower and slower.

We were met on the ground by many Chinese coolies hired to assist us with our supplies. I used several of them to help me, as I had a large trunk of medical supplies. I'll say one thing for the Chinese, they may not be built well in the chest area, but they do have strong legs. This comes from the way they transport their goods. With the use of bamboo sticks and some ropes they hoisted the trunk up, and were off before I could say anything. In the meantime, I had gotten so bad on my walk to the temple, that I began removing all of the equipment I was carrying. My rifle, my pistol belt, anything and everything I could, that would make it easier for me to walk. There were times when I even crawled on hands and knees! At that time I would not have cared if the Japanese had come and shot me. I could easily have helped them. I had never felt so bad in all my life. Fortunately, the Japanese did not arrive even though they had seen us jump in. We were informed by the local people that the Japanese had several small garrisons dispersed around the area we were to operate in.

I slowly made my way to the Buddha Temple. As soon as I arrived the resident priest took me in and gave me a hot bath and hot tea. This was an automatic tonic. It brought me back to normal instantly and when the rest of our people arrived I assisted them with the same treatment. It wasn't long before everyone had arrived and were all treated for heat exhaustion. After that we began the task of securing our headquarters. The first thing I did was to have the water bag filled with 50 gallons of water taken from the stream nearby at the back of the temple. The stream was no more than a few inches wide, but sufficient to give us a good supply of what I hoped would be fresh water. It appeared to be artesian fed and this stream in turn fed into the river that flowed in front of the temple. The river was no place to take water from because I noticed that the small village nearby used to for supplying all of their needs. This included taking the run-off from the rice paddies. From my experience back at the compound, I knew these people fertilized their rice crops with human waste taken from their outhouses. I didn't think the river was even safe for swimming, let alone anything else. As soon as the water bag was filled I placed enough chlorine tablets in it to insure the death of any bacteria that might be on the loose. This had to set several hours before we could consume any amount. The water had a taste about it that reminded the drinker of the local Y.M.C.A. pool back home.

About this time Jim Gardner was putting together his radio as we had to report in to Kumning the result of our drop. The radio had a hand generator. Two men sat facing each other and placed their hands on bicycle type handle bars. This was cranked by the two of them and generated a power sufficient to operate the radio. Of course, the speed had to be maintained in order to insure power enough to keep the signal from fading.

"Keep grinding, keep grinding. Faster, faster, the signal is fading", Jim Gardner yelled.

His interpreter took up the chant to inform the two Chinese working the handles. They had to be constantly chided in order to keep sufficient power flowing to the radio.

"There is no strength in their arms and shoulders", Cheng Chin Yin, my interpreter, would tell us. "They tire too fast".

Jim Gardner yelled at me. "Al, you and Roy take over. I can't hear the code coming in and have a hard time sending what I want". We would then have to relieve the Chinese and keep up a good power flow. It required a lot of grit and stamina to make the current strong. Nevertheless, these jobs were performed and we made periodic contact at designated times so that the Japanese could not trace us or pin-point our location.

Guards were also posted around the camp. This was handled by the Chinese Commandos because they could speak the local language. This always reminded us that we were only in an advisory capacity and the Chinese were the ones that would handle things. We soon learned that they were inadequate for many things and more and more responsibilities were turned over to us. The Chinese were green in many things and they had a difficult time understanding the things we expected of them.

The first night for me was a laugh. When issued a mosquito net back in Kunming, I thought it would be too bulky and unwieldy, so I cut it down to a small piece that would go just over my head. I reasoned that the rest of me would be covered by the clothing I was wearing. Boy! Was I wrong! Because the weather was so hot and muggy, sleeping with clothes on was out of the question. Fortunately, I had one of the coolies haul my parachute from the drop zone, and I was able to rig this to a rafter of the temple and used it like a large tent. I was able to crawl into it and keep the mosquitoes out. But what I also kept in was the heat. Nylon does not breathe. I would have given anything to have had my mosquito net about then. Life in a constant learning process, and the mistakes we make we have to live with.

We had taken a million yen with us. The exchange rate was not a lot in American dollars, but it was enough for our use in the field. This money was to be used by us to purchase the things we needed. This not only included food and lodging, but information and intelligence. The Chinese would sell anything for the right price. One of the first things was to get us a supply of food. We had to live off the land, so the first thing we had to do was to hire some cooks and food handlers. These, of course, come from the local residents. They were very poor and lived with very short rations. This was because the Japanese were taking the bulk of their rice and shipping it back to Japan. Therefore, we paid them well and provided double rations compared to what they were living on. This made them very cooperative and very happy. Because we Americans were in the minority we ate what the Chinese fixed. This consisted of plenty of rice, some vegetables, and a little meat, like chicken and pork. Occasionally we would have fish, but not a lot as it was in short supply. We became rather proficient with chop-sticks and learned to eat like our hosts. Eggs seemed to be the biggest single mainstay for us and we consumed plenty of them. It was a long time after returning home before I could look an egg in the eye.

At the city of Li Tze Sin, where we dropped, there was a farm market. This market contained "fresh meat", but the sight of it was more than the eye could stand. The meat was covered with flies... large buzzing and crawling ones. I quickly informed the cook and officers that we would not eat local meat in that condition. It was agreed that we would carry only live chickens and pigs. Now we had the problem of making sure we had a fenced area to keep our legged acquisitions. One man was given the responsibility of providing such a place. Several of us were watching him from the balcony of the temple. He had stolen some wire mesh and to secure the corners he found several bamboo stakes. In order to drive them into the ground he picked up a rifle grenade. To him it looked like a fine instrument for the purpose of pounding. All of us watching this began to yell at him. He looked up with a

76

fine wide grin thinking we were urging him on. We finally got the attention of one of the interpreters who stopped him from what could have been an explosive experience. We were learning to cope with new challenges.

When food was prepared large pots were used. When a chicken was to be used the entire body was cut up. Fortunately, the feathers and entrails were removed. Everything else was put to use, including the head and feet. Rice was the first thing taken. This was scraped into a bowl, and from a communal pot one would remove chicken meat. This was then placed in the bowl of rice and was scooped in to your mouth. Rather than sit at tables, we all crouched around the pot. The meals were completely different than those served in the Chinese restaurants back home. There were no table manners. Everyone reached a grabbed as needed.

Our Buddha Temple sat in a very pretty area. Small mountains surrounded us with a fast running river going past the front of the temple. A small foot bridge crossed it that carried traffic into the town of Li Tze Sin. This was the hub of activity where the women would exchange gossip, do their laundry in the river and watch their children play. This was also where the men conducted business among themselves and offered their wares for sale. Set apart from the rest of the world, as they were, they functioned as they had for many thousands of years. It was a quaint setting. The war, by and large, had not affected them and we hoped to keep it that way.

The river presented an interesting place for our men to bathe and horse-play. I tried my best to discourage the use of the river, only because it was so polluted. With the help of Rudy Dolozal I had run a bamboo pipe from the small creek that fed this river. This we piped into the temple, and with the use of some discarded cans we fashioned a shower that served the purpose of keeping the body clean. My fear was that sitting or swimming in the river would cause a parasitic worm that was common in this part of China, to enter the body causing more problems than we needed. As it was, dysentery and diarrhea were beginning to show up. While we were in camp I began noticing that several of the Chinese Commandos were listless and feverish. Knowing that worms were a constant problem for these people, I began a series of I.V. shots to kill the parasite. Worm medicine was included in my trunk of supplies. I found these shots worked wonders and the men were back to health shortly.

One day Capt. Cook asked Roy Gallant, Jim Gardner, Rudy Dolozal and me to go with him. He wanted to visit the village of Hung La Mao. This was located 5 to 6 miles south and west of our headquarters. We were looking for information about Japanese troops and activities in the area. I asked my interpreter, Chang Chin Yin, to go along. We had become good friends and were not separated very often. The "roads" leading to Hung La Mao consisted of nothing more than paths between rice paddies. With the aid of local peasants we covered the distance by mid-morning and entered the small town, to be greeted by the locals with stares of disbelief. Most had never seen an American, and many did not realize that a war was going on. They called us "Megwo-Ping', meaning American Soldier. Our visit produced little information, other than that the Japanese were stationed at several places within a 10 to 15 mile radius. We did find out that the "Grape-vine" communication method of the Chinese provided the Japanese with information on our activities. This would prove difficult for us as time went on. I wondered sometimes how we ever got out alive.

One of the interesting things in Hung La Mao was the stores. The merchants offered silks and figurines and all sorts of stones for sale. This is where I should have purchased everything I could have carried, but it was impossible to do anything because of the nature of our business. But then again,

I knew so little of the value of things at that age.

One place I was taken to with my interpreter was a clinic. These people were desperate for medicines and bandages. When they heard that I was a medic, they figured I was able to heal the illnesses of the entire town. The two of us viewed the sick and ailing and promised to radio for medicine and other necessities. When we returned to camp Jim Gardner did send a list of things I had worked up, but we never did receive anything. It was all too obvious that weapons and other related items took preference here.

One day we were enjoying ourselves around camp when we noticed a tattered form approaching from the west. He had the appearance of an American but at that distance we could not be sure. Our curiosity was piqued until he began his final approach across the bridge leading to our camp. Yes, he was an American, we could see that now. He staggered into camp and we knew something was not right. What was an American doing way out here? We knew we had not lost anyone. Everyone began asking him questions, and we found out that he was one of Merrill's Marauders. This was a group of volunteers, like us, that operated in China and Asia. They would go out in small groups, generally on foot, to ambush and harass the Japanese. On one of these raids, this man told us, he had been captured but escaped again and was on his way back to the main lines and his own people. Having heard we were in the area, he looked us up. He spent several days with us resting and getting back his strength. We respected this man very much. After about a week, he decided he should try to find his way back to his own camp. We regretted seeing him go, but we understood his desire to leave. After providing him with several maps of the area, as well as money, we shook hands and he was off. We often wondered if he made it.

Before any Operational group jumps into the field, a Jedburgh team goes in one or two months before in order to prepare for their arrival. A Jedburgh team consists of an officer and an enlisted radio man. These men have the difficult task of setting things up and staying out of the way of the enemy. Sometimes they are lost before they can complete their mission. We had a team before we jumped into France and now before we jumped into China. This had its advantages as well as disadvantages. The advantage is that we know what to expect and where we are going to stay while in the field. Being discovered by the enemy because someone has let it slip, was a definite disadvantage.

The man that set this all up, because he was in the area, paid us a visit. He wanted to make sure everything went all right. We had the honor of his visit. First Lt. Rickerson was our Jedburgh man and one day he walked into camp with his radio operator interpreter. He casually asked if I would dress his wound. I agreed and he took off his shirt. The wound was in his back.

"How did you get this?" I asked with obvious surprise and alarm.

He quietly replied, "I ran into a small squad of Japanese led by an officer. We killed the entire squad except the officer. I was about to take a bead on him, when my M-I jammed. The man raised his Samurai sword to try and sever my head from the rest of me, so I raised my rifle to ward off the blow. This did the trick but the tip of his sword came down and caught me in the back. The fortunate part was that the blow unjammed my gun and I was able to finish him off."

Lt. Rickerson was left wounded and bleeding and this is how he showed up in camp. His radio man had placed a bandage on the wound and they headed for us. It didn't take long before I had him sewn up and bandaged properly. He remained with us several days so I could keep changing the dressings and checking the wound for infection. He even stayed with us and participated in our upcoming battle.

Chapter X

Captain Cook and the officers met with General Wong, the guerrilla leaders in our area, and General Chiang, the 10th. Chinese Army leader and several smaller groups. This meeting was necessary in order to establish a plan to wipe out the outpost located at Tai Yuan Tze, which was the thorn in our side. This force had to be eliminated in order to cut the Japanese supply lines. This enemy force was also responsible for the removal of large quantities of rice to Japan. This was our mission and this we had to put a stop to.

As the crow flies, Tai Yuan Tze was about 12 miles distance. There were no roads in the area, only narrow paths between the rice paddies, and walking was the only way we could get there. This meant the trip would cover about 20 to 25 miles one way. So on August 4th we set out. It was now about 8 days since we had jumped in.

Now, rice paddy walking is tricky. The paths are one to two feet wide at the most. Passing is next to impossible, except for one person stepping into the paddy as the other one passes. This also includes the proper bowing and salutation before the pass can be completed. Keeping your foot from mashing down the side of the paddy wall was always a concern for us. If this was done the water contained in each paddy would break through and drain its contents, resulting in the loss of that amount of rice production. Even though many things were expendable during war, we did not want to create additional problems for an already poor nation.

Everything had to be carried by coolie. We paid them well for their services because we felt we could get the most in return for our dollar spent. We did find out that no matter where you are, someone had figured out a way to make a lot of money without a lot of effort. It wasn't long down the rice paddy highway that a shout came down the line that the Japanese were advancing. It was then the order came that we should scatter and hide in the cover along the edges and wait for the Jap Patrol. At this point we happened to be an area that was quite hilly. A small stand of bamboo trees and scrub oak skirted the path. This made for good concealment and we dove for cover. Coolies were running everywhere; some with heavy loads, others with lighter weights. All of them using the "pogo-sticks" with baskets attached to the ends. The baskets all bounced with the rhythm of their walking.

One of the coolies was carrying two baskets of Chinese money. This money was to be used by us to purchase information on Japanese movements, as well as to pay our room and board. As we should have guessed, the Japanese Patrol was false and the coolies with the money were gone. There in an old saying that a fool and his money are soon parted, and we sure became the fools. After pooling what money we could scrape up among us we preceded on our way.

It was our plan to attack the Japanese in two days' time with a surprise attack at dawn. This required an overnight rest. We chose to rest at the small village of Ho Chang Ton. When we entered the village we were surprised to see a Chinese hanging by his thumbs in the village square, with his feet barely touching the ground. Upon asking about the problem, we were told he had been found collaborating with the Japanese. Collaborating was common, but punishment like this was not. We supposed they were trying to impress us with their loyalty.

While the officers were conferring with the village leaders and the officers of various guerrilla forces, I was taken to a small hut where several wounded and sick were kept. Recent encounters with the Japanese had left several of them in need of treatment. The medical supplies I had with me were sufficient to take care of their needs. Even the administration of an American aspirin tablet seemed to work wonders.

While I was doing this, a plan was being devised. Two of our Chinese officers were disguised as coolies and were sent with the group that daily supplied the Japanese garrison. Their primary function was to survey the outpost and to prepare a map of the garrison and surrounding area. When they returned they were to brief us on these things; this would give us the latest information so we would not be in the dark when we attacked. Because it was late that day and we were only a few miles from our intended attack on the Japanese, we were allowed the use of a small hut in which to spend a couple of hours in sleep. The rest of the Chinese commandos were scattered around the village. We awoke around midnight, and after a few bowls of rice and some hot tea, we began our advancement toward the Japanese outpost. We were informed that the outpost was manned by 200 to 300 Japanese troops, armed with rifles, light and heavy machine guns, light and heavy mortars and one artillery piece.

It was early morning and light was just beginning to appear in the East when we come over a slight rise in the ground. The bulk of the rice paddies had thinned out leaving sandy hills covered by some vegetation that offered little concealment. A few scrubby trees and a few stands of bamboo were visible. After cresting a slight rise we could see quite a distance. The sun was now in full view, and looking ahead we could see that the outpost was defended by pillboxes and trenches and caves, in which the Japanese had hidden themselves. This was now the morning of the 5th of August.

With the commando training our Chinese had received, and the superior weapons we carried, it was our lot to be chosen to attack the heavily defended frontal area. General Wong was to attack the flanks with an additional 200 guerrillas and blow up a bridge over which an escape could be made by the Japanese. The smaller units of Chinese guerrillas were sent to ambush any Japanese re-enforcements from a larger garrison about four hours walk away. General Chiang was also to operate on the flanks, providing additional aid to any area that required it, and giving back-up to repel counter attacks by the Japanese.

Coming over this small rise in the ground, we entered a slight depression that was flanked on two sides by a small hill or dune shaped terrain. A few dried rice paddies lay before us on the right flank. We thought we had traveled with a certain amount of secrecy, but it was obvious the Japanese knew of our arrival and the size of our forces. We were told later, after the war had ended, by the Japanese commander that he knew all about us before we attacked him. This had allowed him time to re-enforce his position. We were now facing more than a thousand enemy soldiers.

Upon making the approach, we reached a point where the mortars and demolition men, under 1st. Lt. Larry Drew, left the main body and proceeded South and East to high ground. From that point his mortar squad was to be able to see the garrison and could place mortars on the slopes opposite from the rest of us. This was to create two fronts for the Japanese to contend with. The entire operation was not to begin until Captain Cook would fire a red flare to signal the beginning. This would allow Lt. Drew to be about a mile from our main line.

It was just breaking light in the East when Lt. Drew led his men across country, but before he could reach any recognizable vantage point Captain Cook shot off his flare that lit the sky and began the battle. Larry had run into terrain difficulty that slowed him down. We began our attack with heavy firing. Larry could see the tracers and hear the firing, but was not in a good position. After breaking into a run he and his men reached a low rise, from which they could see the enemy side of the garrison that we were assaulting.

"Come on Johnny", Sgt. VanTimmeran yelled at me and we took off to the right. I supposed he planned a flanking movement. A lot the two of us could do. But, Van out-ranked me and I scurried after him. We had no sooner reached a dry rice paddy when we both heard a burst of fire close by. We hit the dirt like we were tackled. Bullets picked up small pieces of dirt from the rice paddy, just over our heads. We lay perfectly still. This was a fine thing; we just got here and they were shooting at us. Neither fear nor panic entered our minds, but we both agreed it was not an ideal place to stay.

After what seemed a long time, Van said, "Johnny, we have to get out of here. We're too much in the open."

"You're telling me?" I agreed. Van's response was encouraging.

He said, "As soon as the Japanese let up on us, I am making a run for it to that rise over there. Be sure to follow as soon as you can."

"Don't worry old boy", I responded, "You aren't leaving me here alone. This was your idea, I'm not staying here."

I saw Van rise, slowly at first, but then with a burst of speed he took off. I figured if the Japanese were watching they may be surprised enough and hesitate long enough for me to go also. That is just what I did. I rose fast and my long skinny legs pumped like pistons, propelling me after him. We both hit the ground below the large rise. After looking around, found the rest of our men crouched down waiting for the command to advance.

Captain Cook's flare had gone off and this is when everything began to happen. We were with the main force of American and Chinese commandos. David Boak, our 50 Cal. machine gunner, had set up his weapon on a hill overlooking the field of fire. This was one of the guns we expected the Japanese would take out of operation right away. The odds were against us but we had to hit hard and fast and get out of there as soon as possible.

Now the Japanese were putting their mortars into action, and were famous for laying shells into an object in just three shots. You could hear the whistle of the mortars as they came through the air. You couldn't see them because of the speed they traveled. It was impossible, from our position, to determine where they came from, but you could hear the ominous whistle and knew they would land nearby. The Japanese began loping shells into the troops behind the small rise they had taken to for protection. Some of the Chinese had been hit and I, as the only medic, had my work cut out for me. I was on my way to the first line of troops when a mortar shell hit about 100 feet ahead of me. One of the Chinese soldiers was hit and bounced about 10 feet in the air and hit the ground. He was lying there with a large chunk blown out of his behind. I bandaged the man and did what I could for him and the others that were hit and directed them, through my interpreter, to go back out of the line of fire. Things were happening so fast that I lost track of Van. We lost twelve Chinese, three dead and nine wounded before we withdrew and finally pulled out. Those that were killed were left where they had fallen. An old Chinese custom says that the last one to touch a dead person was the one that had to bury him. Needless to say, no one wanted this responsibility.

As all this was taking place, Jim Gardner came over the hill looking for water. His canteen had been shot and he lost the contents. One gets thirsty under these conditions and Jim helped himself to the canteen of one of the dead soldiers, and then slowly made his way back out of the line of fire. It wasn't until later that I found out where Jim had been.

He told me, after we had a time to reflect on things, that he had been with Lt. Drew and Lt. Whitney where they had positioned the Chinese mortar men, on a low protected side of the position. Lt. Drew had taken Sgt. Miller with him to the brow of the hill so they could observe the enemy and place shells in the most productive spot. Larry Drew said to Hob Miller, "We will fire about 30 degrees to the East, while we range in on the garrison. When we have the range, we'll shift and fire in the actual position. In this way we'll avoid firing on Capt. Cook and his men."

Hob Miller was left there to set up his mortar while Larry went back to his other mortar squad. Hob was now alone and vulnerable. The Japanese had placed snipers in trees and one of them took a bead on Hob, sending a bullet through his stomach. Philip, Larry's interpreter, who had at the same time wondered across Hob, came running back to Larry shouting, "Miller's been shot, Miller's been hit and he's down." Instantly, Larry broke away from his squad and crawled to where Miller lay.

"I'm hit --- pretty bad." he gasped out, gritting his teeth.

"Don't move Hob," Lt Drew shouted to him. "I'm on my way." At this point Larry grasped him under the armpits and dragged him down the safe side of the hill. This is where Lt. Whitney and Sgt. Dolozal were laying out demolitions.

"You'll have to take care of him", Larry shouted to Whitney, "Find his wound, bandage him and see that he gets back to Johnson. I have to get back to my squad and the mortars".

Captain Cook was having difficulty with his Chinese troops in the frontal attack position. He could not make headway. Preventing him were the Japanese machine gun and mortar emplacements directly ahead of him. Because Larry Drew was located near these emplacements, Roy Gallant and Jim Gardner were sent to him, along with several Chinese commandos, as well as an interpreter we called "Spanky". He took his name from the "Our Gang Comedies" we had seen back home, because he looked so much like the character.

Taking out the machine gun nest meant going over the top of the dune type hill we were hiding behind, and down the other side into a small valley, and then up again the other side of the depression. This left the squad in a very vulnerable spot. Upon arriving on the valley floor, Jim and Roy could see the Japanese emplacements rising up above them. The placing of a hand grenade would be the only way to put the machine gun out of business.

Roy and Jim jumped down into the deep grassed over ditch, along with Spanky. Between Roy and Jim were several Chinese commandos. One of them kept putting his head up to see what was happening. The first thing you should learn in combat in to not be too curious. After all, this is not a trip to the circus. You should not be like a tourist, trying to take in all of the sights. This particular chap took one too many looks and was shot in the head by a Jap sniper. Many of them were discovered in the trees but eventually all were eliminated, or at least that is what we thought.

After the Chinese was shot, Roy and Jim retreated to a small shack about 150 feet from the pillbox where the machine gun was located. Here they waited for Lt. Drew to give further orders. The pillbox was a small mounded structure of cement, re-enforced with metal, and had small slits in the face of it that allowed the Japanese to fire at us without being hit themselves. Roy had been carrying his Thompson Sub-machine gun and had been firing it for some time without damaging the pillbox. Lt. Drew arrived and said to Roy, "That pillbox has to go. It's causing us too much trouble."

Roy was always a quiet fellow. He came from Maine where he worked as a lumberjack. He was massively built and kept pretty much to himself. His response was always matter-of-fact, and was by and large passive in his actions. He didn't respond right away, except for a glance at the pillbox and then back again to Lt. Drew. He quietly said, "If Jim goes with me, and about four other Chinese commandos I figure I could get the job done."

Jamming a full clip of rounds in his Thompson, and looking over at Jim, Roy left Larry standing at the shack and headed out to complete the task. Before Roy tried to take the pillbox, he circled around behind it to see how many Japanese were in the area. To his great surprise, he saw a goodly number had dug fox holes and many were beginning to advance toward us. After determining the strength of the enemy, Roy and Jim took their Chinese and crawled up as close to the pillbox as they could get without being seen. Because the slits were so small, Roy was afraid he could not slip a grenade inside. Just as Roy was about to make his first attempt, a Japanese face appeared staring at Jim through the slit. Capt. Cook had been watching the whole action of Roy and Jim from back at the dune where I was attending the wounded. When he noticed the face in the slit, he placed an accurate shot, killing the Japanese and saving Jim's life. All of this confusion allowed Roy to sneak close enough and drop the grenade inside the pillbox. After a few seconds he heard a muffled thud. Just to make sure, he slid another one in. This took a few seconds too long and Roy received a shot from a sniper's gun. Those that we had killed before were replaced by others. Roy was hit in the shoulder, but the sniper was killed by Jim Gardner who was near Roy at the time. Lt. Raf Hirtz had come upon the scene…and between him and Jim, they were able to bring Roy back to where I was standing.

Now that Hob Miller was transferred to the rear, Larry Drew made his way back to the spot Miller had been occupying, keeping as low a profile as possible. Here he finished setting up the mortar Miller had been working on. The first shot Larry sent off was at 30 degrees off our main assault, led by Cpt. Cook. This first round went upward, arched beautifully and come down with a loud "whump" of explosion. Nothing could be seen. The range was too far. So the range for the second round was cut in half. The same visual sight was made following the round's release. Still nothing could be seen of the impact. After cutting it in half two more times, Larry's mortar was now hitting at one-eighth of a mile from us.

We all wondered where our Chinese guerrilla army was located. Larry Drew happened to glance back over his shoulder and there was Gen. Wong, and his army, about a mile to the rear. They were of little help and furnished no fighting to relieve us. They were watching at a safe distance. This appeared to be typical of the Chinese as I witnessed Capt. Cook holding a 45 Cal. pistol to the head of several Chinese commandos, forcing them to go into battle.

Swinging the mortar's direction 30 degrees to the west, and cutting down the range even further, it was now easy for Larry to place shots right in the main fortifications, causing much havoc and destruction. Leaving this mortar to be handled by the Chinese, Lt. Drew now set up the second mortar facing the direction which the shots had come from that wounded Hob Miller. Drew had been receiving continuous fire from his right, but by keeping low had been protected. He now looked in that direction and saw that if he had not stopped when he did, he would have walked straight into the Japanese trenches which protected the South perimeter of the garrison.

Sgt. Dolozal, who had been helping Lt. Whitney with Miller, joined Larry Drew on the mortars. This also allowed Rudy Dolozal to deliver rifle fire directly into the trenches, thus keeping the Japanese under cover so that Larry could make good use of the mortar. According to Larry, he and Rudy had great sport. While Dolozal kept the Japanese heads low with rifle fire, Larry was able to drop round after round into the enemy trenches.

When Roy and Hob were finally brought to me, I administered a shot of morphine to each of them. Roy had been shot through the muscle on the top of the shoulder. The bullet had gone through without hitting the large sub-clavian artery. He was fortunate - he could have bled to death if this had been severed. Hob Miller was not so fortunate. His wound left him immobile. Because the bullet had exited Hob's back and had taken a path through his lungs, I made a patch from part of a poncho. This I taped over the opening so that Hob would be able to breathe without taking air into his lungs from the outside. This prevented the lung from collapsing. Next, we formed a stretcher from bamboo poles lashed together with jackets from some of the men, and placed Hob on this so he could be carried back to camp.

The help that was supposed to be given to us by Gen. Wong and Gen. Chiang was virtually non-existent. The overwhelming odds against us must have discouraged our allies. They were nowhere to be found.

The Japanese were getting too close with their mortars and we figured they were preparing to counter attack. The best part of valor was a little discretion. Capt. Cook was making plans to withdraw. He was using his walkie-talkie to advise the mortar and demolition squads to prepare to withdraw. Lt. Drew and Lt. Whitney were advised to retrace their steps as we were going to leave. Miller was placed on the litter we had fashioned and off we went. We used four-man teams of Chinese soldiers to carry the litter. Going over the path with the litter was tricky. In some areas we had to shift to two-man teams as the path between the rice paddies was too narrow for two men abreast.

Roy, being an ex-lumberjack and strong as a bull, was able to make his way back under his own power. The Buddha Temple was about 25 miles away, but we made it in spite of the hardships we had to put up with. The trip down, the lack of sleep and the battle tensions we had gone through, left us very weary. In spite of all this we made it back without incident. We had a total of two wounded Americans and nine Chinese casualties. We left the Japanese with an estimated 50 dead or wounded. We had done well.

Upon arriving back at our Buddha Temple we posted guards. The Japanese could have followed us and we didn't want to take the chance of being caught unawares. The Chinese wounded were set aside in one of the small (ante rooms) off the main area where we were staying. This provided a sick bay, or hospital ward, where I could take care of them. Upon inspecting their wounds I found several that were very serious. I did everything I could for them by applying sulfa drugs and bandages to their wounds. I had some difficulty with this because some of them wanted treatment to be performed by the local priest. Many of the 'treatments' were no more than handed down methods that included a certain amount of ritual that had little or no value in healing. I had placed Roy and Hob on the balcony so I could keep an eye on them day and night.

It was now August 6th and we were making plans to evacuate our wounded. Before we could complete our plans, several of the Chinese that were badly wounded died. Because they were Buddhists, the temple priests took over the last rites. These last rites included the ringing of the temple bells and the burning of incense. A constant 24 hour ringing of the enormous bell in the tower kept us awake the entire time. There are even times yet, that certain incense smells will recall these episodes in China. The fragrance seemed to penetrate everything. The constant gong of the bell filled our every movement and thought. We could not get away from it. At night we would eventually drop off into a fitful sleep, but were sub-consciously aware of every toll of the bell. There must have been a prescribed number of days that had to be filled before the bell finally ceased to disturb our activities. Even when it stopped ringing we could still feel the vibrations.

A message was coming through on the radio... an atomic bomb had been dropped on Japan. Jim Gardner, our radio man, kept repeating the words in disbelief. "The war is over - the war is over," he kept saying. All of us thought he was joking until it finally sank in that what he heard was in fact, the truth. We were all jubilant and ready to celebrate with another bowl of rice. This all took on another shade of despair when we read further in the message to find out that we had to stay on and be ready to extend our activities for an additional 30 days. The Japanese in the interior were not ready to give up. Wouldn't you know it? Our war was to last an additional 30 days longer than everyone else. We could be killed during a time when peace was established. None of us were extremely happy.

Now something had to be done. We had to leave the Buddha Temple. It was too risky to stay where Japanese troops could retaliate. It so happened that my interpreter was engaged to marry the daughter of a man who owned and ruled a small town north of Li Tze Sin, called Tan Kawn Chiao. This was also the headquarters of Gen. Wong. We headed for it with all expediency. Gen. Wong's headquarters had a small landing strip that we could use to get our buddies out to a hospital. We all stayed in the house of my interpreter's future father-in-law, who had a large home that could accommodate the Americans. He also provided us with food and basic necessities while we were there. While we were staying here in Tan Kawn Chiao, Cheng Chin Yin, made preparations for his wedding. A festive air was prevalent and a local hall was made ready for the wedding feast. All of us Americans were invited, together with all of the prominent local people, as well as many of the bride's friends. A rather large group was assembled and food in abundance was made ready. This became an experience only a few of us ever saw again. Here we were, 600 miles into Japanese-held territory, and we were having a wedding feast that would probably not be repeated for some time by any of the Chinese. It was safe to assume that when the Communists took over, wealthy displays like this would be stopped. My good friend Cheng Chin Yin would have a short honeymoon. He was still in the service and we had to prepare for our return to Kunming. I often wondered if he ever made it back to his bride. There was so much confusion and killing after we had returned to Kunming. Our weapons were taken away from us and we were confined to our compound until finally orders arrived for our departure. All during the days and nights we could hear shooting and artillery going off in the area surrounding us.

It was now almost a week since we had attacked the Japanese. Roy and Hob needed good medical attention - something more than I could give them in the field. Jim Gardner had set up his radio and was asking that a doctor be sent in. This was early in the morning of the 12th of August, and by that afternoon we heard the drone of a C-47 airplane coming in. Out popped a parachute and Dr. Agee arrived from our compound back in Kunming. This was his first and only jump. He had never had any practice jumps before, and we found out from him that it was something he did not enjoy.

Dr. Agee took over the treatment of the two wounded Americans, and with my help they were loaded onto a small L-5, or Piper Cub airplane, the following day. We had to arrange for this small plane to fly in. The field was not large enough for the C-47 to land. This small plane was equipped for medical evacuation, but had a short range. Extra gas had to be taken along and fed to the engines so the trip could be made. The two men and Dr. Agee soon left and we watched them as they flew out of sight.

CHAPTER XI

Radio contact with Kunming told us that the Japanese were finally giving up. Many of them, we were told, were arriving at the city of Hengyeng. Our orders were to proceed there and to assist where possible in the surrender of these troops. Before starting out, two re-supply drops were made to us in order to replenish the ammunition stocks we had used. With the uncertainty of things, we did not want to be caught short. Enroute to Hengyeng, Japanese garrisons were contacted with surrender demands. We had jumped into the middle of several outposts, and now we had to go through them to get to Hengyeng. Our requests were answered by the Japanese saying they did not have orders to surrender, and they were ready to continue fighting.

As the days moved on, the Japanese finally agreed to surrender to the Regular Chinese Army. It complicated things when Gen. Wong of the guerrillas insisted the Japanese surrender to him. He proved to be a difficult person to deal with, and in time he showed his true colors. He was definitely a communist.

We finally arrived in Hengyeng, despite being harassed by the Chinese guerrillas and some bandits who wanted our weapons and equipment. Upon arriving in Hengyeng our Chinese commandos were attached to the 4th Chinese Command, and all but five of our own men were sent back to Kunming. Maj. Cook, Lt. Whitney, Sgt. VanTimmeran, Sgt. Dolozal, Sgt. Gardner, and Sgt. Johnson remained. We had all received promotions. Our job now was to see that our weapons, radios, and medical supplies were placed in the proper hands. We had now located a large building near the waterfront in Hengyeng, and retaining our interpreters, were living like kings. The five of us remained for about two more weeks, making arrangements for the transfer of our materials to the Chinese army. At every step in the process we were confronted by the guerrilla leaders to turn everything over to them. Even threats of bodily harm were used, but to no avail.

We had occupied the upper floor of the building which had a large verandah extending on three sides. The lower floor was used for storage by the Chinese. We hoped the upper floor would provide enough protection from looting by the locals, and would give us an edge in case we were attacked by the guerrillas. In one sense we were prisoners of the Chinese, even though we were not restrained. Sides were being chosen, for or against the Communists, and we were in the way.

Several times I had made trips into parts of Hengyeng to attend some sick person. Getting there was very exciting! The only available transportation was by sampan. We would arrive at the waterfront loaded with medical supplies, and then make the necessary negotiations with the boat people to get someone to take us to the other side of the river. At the city of Hengyeng the river became a good-sized body of water. Several large junks were used in the river at this point and many small sampans plied the waters with a wide assortment of wares and people. Just a few bridges were built over the Siang River, on which the city of Hengyeng was built. Besides, going by sampan was a lot more exciting than walking the bridge. There was little I could do for these helpless Chinese civilians. I did hand out pills, mostly aspirin, and applied some dressings when I felt it would be of help. I remember one woman that could not swallow without a lot of pain. After checking, I figured she was suffering from a cancer and even the aspirin I could offer did no more than help her psychologically. Chang Chin Yin, my medical interpreter, helped me tremendously, and we did everything we could under those primitive conditions. For all my effort, Chang was able to get me an honorary commission as Colonel in the Chinese Nationalist Army. I felt this to be a great honor, as I was the only one to be so chosen.

CHAPTER XII

The days dragged slowly by but finally, after many radio contacts with Kunming, the airport outside Hengyeng was made available to us, and we were informed that we would be picked up and returned to Kunming the following day. It was now around the 23rd of August, and during these past two weeks the Japanese had been arriving in Hengyeng by the hundreds and thousands. Wherever we went there were marching Japanese troops, many of them with their weapons. This felt a little strange...five Americans and thousands of Japanese. We didn't mind the odds against us. After all, this was the way it always worked, but this was a bit scary.

As promised, the very next day a B-46 transport was sent in and we boarded with little delay. Before I finally entered the plane, Chang handed me a small package. Upon opening it I found a jade tear-drop pendent. I was most grateful as I had always valued this particular stone. With it was a promise that he would send a jade Buddha statue when he arrived at his home. I never received this. I could understand why, because it wasn't long before the Communists took over China. He probably lost everything. Because he was an intellectual, he may have lost his life also.

After returning to Kunming, we were again sent to our compound outside of the city. It was sure good to be back in a familiar setting again. It was almost like being home. It wasn't long after returning that our personal weapons were taken from us, and we were confined to quarters until our flight back to Calcutta, India. The Communists were beginning their takeover in earnest. We could hear cannon and small arms firing in the distance. At night the fighting seemed to be the heaviest. We were at their mercy and none of us felt at ease. When the news came that we were to leave, we were all very happy to go. We had had enough of war and all the stupid things that go along with it.

Many of us were ill when we returned to Calcutta. Living in China for a year did us no good. Dysentery and yellow jaundice were common ailments. Malaria was present also but the use of Atabrine kept this in line. Many reported to sick-call and were treated. Some were sent to hospitals and treated or sent aboard ship for home and spent their time in sick-bay.

Being the last of our operational group to return, we spent a month in Calcutta waiting for transportation back to the States. During this time I was able to see a lot of sights. The things denied me on my arrival were now made available. The bazaar of Calcutta was the most fascinating. It was just as I had supposed it to be from seeing movies of such places; long, darkly lit, avenues of merchants hawking wares and displaying items. Smells of things being cooked and fried wafted in the air you breathed and, with merchants grabbing at your sleeves, it made you feel that you were part of another world. I am sure their hope was to separate you from every dollar you had brought along.

My interest was in a sapphire. I knew they would be costly, but I was prepared as I had taken a goodly amount of American dollars along. This money had come from the sale of cartons of cigarettes and chocolate bars. While we were in Kunming I had taken the rations that I had accumulated while in the field, and paid a visit to the black market. Chang Chin Yin had contacts in that area also, and I was able to set up a meeting with one of the shady fellows that could offer me a nice price. This was illegal of course but I was able, with the help of Chang, to circumvent the Military Police. I made my deal in American dollars. I was not about to take Chinese money that had a questionable value. The meeting took place in an area that was off-limits to Americans. We went down a long, dark alley between rows of dingy dwellings. It was a good thing I had Chang with me, because alone I would not have made it back in one piece. With my eyes constantly peeled for the appearance of the M.P.'s, I made the deal and came out with what I thought was good. That deal, coupled with my back pay, provided the funds necessary to make a good stone selection. I finally settled on an item completely different than what I had set out to buy. Being taught at home to be considerate of others, I settled on a silver compact for my sister and a cigarette lighter and case, made of silver, for my father. Both were inset with ruby chips. I never did buy myself anything, as I had run out of money at this time.

Waiting around became boring. We had seen enough of the East and were ready to make our way home. Finally word came that we were to leave and were sent to the docks to board the ship Joseph Hale. It was a fast uneventful trip to Seattle, Washington. We were all anxious to return home, worn and weary and older than when this whole business had started. What would we do, who would we become. Many thoughts entered our minds. We discussed our past and what was ahead for us. Schooling - jobs - work. So many things to plan. It didn't take long before we arrived in the States and were immediately sent by rail to Camp Meade, Md. There we were processed and discharged and on our way home to yet another time in our lives.

We had been given a job and had done it well ... not just an ordinary assignment, but one that brought a small group of men together to penetrate the enemy lines many hundreds of miles. We learned to live under the noses of the enemy to create an organization that could work underground, to live off the land, and to cause large-scale damage, not only to material things but also to psychologically impair the enemy so that he was unable to function effectively. We were ordinary men with ordinary backgrounds doing an extraordinary job under very difficult circumstances.

Author Biography

Al Johnson was born July 5, 1923 in a Military Hospital in the Cincinnati, Ohio area. Shorty after his birth his parents, John and Marie Johnson moved the family to Allegan, Michigan. The family included Al, older brother John and younger sister Marie. The family lived in Allegan and Holland before moving to Grand Rapids. There was some time spent in Lake Odessa but the family returned to Grand Rapids and Al graduated from Central High School in Grand Rapids in 1942.

Al was wondering what to do with his life when he received his draft notice from the United States Army in 1943 so he thought serving in the Military, as his father had done, would be a good place to start. This book is about those years.

When he returned home from his wartime adventures, he attended Grand Rapids Junior College, now Community College, and earned his Associate Degree after two years. Al began a career in sales; first for Oliver Machinery Company in Grand Rapids and then he had an opportunity to work for Crown Beauty Supply where he worked until his retirement.

Al married Jean DeBoer after his Junior College days on August 9, 1947 they have two children; Nancy Moseler born in 1950 and Jim born in 1953. They have seven grandchildren and nine great grand children.

Al, now 96 years old and Jean, who is 98 years old, still live in their own home in Hudsonville Michigan.

The Appendix

After a long wait, World War II spy service honored for daring acts that helped secure Allied victory

By **Missy Ryan**

March 28, 2018

For former military pilot John Billings, the commendation he received on Capitol Hill last week was welcome but late. Seventy-three years late, to be exact.

In February 1945, Billings, flying on behalf of the Office of Strategic Services (OSS), the World War II-era precursor to the CIA, signed up for what seemed like a suicide mission. Fly deep behind Nazi lines, high in the wintry Alps, his superiors asked, to drop a group of covert operatives on a frozen lake. The operation was so perilous the Royal Air Force refused it.

But Billings said yes, and the mission was a success, helping to provide critical information on enemy movements during the war's final period.

Last week, Billings was among about 20 OSS veterans who gathered in Washington as lawmakers including House Speaker Paul D. Ryan (R-Wis.) and Senate Majority Leader Mitch McConnell (R-Ky.) awarded the OSS with the Congressional Gold Medal, the highest civilian honor given by Congress.

The ceremony capped a years-long campaign to secure congressional recognition for the wartime spies who risked their lives to secure an Allied victory. Since at least 2013, advocates of the OSS veterans have been seeking to ensure the service would be recognized as a keystone of the modern U.S. intelligence operation. A bill to that effect, originally introduced in 2013, was stalled for several years in the House. It was introduced again in 2015, and passed in the fall of 2016.

Some 100 to 200 former members of the OSS, which employed about 13,000 civilians and service members at its height, are believed to be alive, but the ranks of surviving veterans are dwindling.

"I'm happy that the OSS got recognized," said Billings, who remains an avid pilot at 94. But, he added: "So many people, deserving people, are not here anymore. It would have been nice to have them know about it, as well."

The OSS was founded in 1942 by William "Wild Bill" Donovan, a distinguished World War I veteran and politician, to help the United States boost its espionage efforts against the Axis powers. Until its dissolution in 1945, it employed thousands of research analysts and dispatched guerrilla operatives on dangerous missions overseas.

The service's Special Operations Branch activities included parachuting into France to support the assault on Normandy and working with Kachin tribesmen in modern-day Burma to gather intelligence on Japanese forces.

At the ceremony last week, Rep. Marcy Kaptur (D-Ohio) spoke with emotion as she recalled the OSS service of her uncle, Cpl. Anthony Rogowski of Toledo. She read from partially censored letters that her Uncle Tony had written while conducting secret operations from an unidentified location in Asia, describing the "pure hell" he encountered as he ferried military assets over remote and mountainous roads.

Marion Frieswyk joined the OSS after geographer Arthur Robinson identified her and another young graduate student, her future husband Henry Frieswyk, during a summer course. The pair moved to Washington and began helping the service build maps and topographic models used by military and government leaders. After the OSS was shut down, both joined the CIA. Marion Frieswyk left the agency in the 1950s while her husband retired in 1980 after becoming head of the cartography division.

"It was a very hush-hush time," Frieswyk, 96, said of her years working in intelligence. "My children didn't even know where we worked."

In a statement, CIA spokeswoman Heather Fritz Horniak said the medal was "fitting recognition for the exceptionally talented, courageous, and resourceful OSS officers who rose to the challenge" during World War II.

DIA receives OSS Congressional Gold Medal

By Chris Van Dam and Jordan Bishop, DIA Public Affairs

Joint Base Anacostia-Bolling, Aug. 7, 2019 —
    The Defense Intelligence Agency received the Office of Strategic Services Congressional Gold Medal Award during a ceremony held at DIA Headquarters, July 31.
    The OSS Society, the organization responsible for honoring the historic accomplishments of the OSS during World War II, awarded DIA in recognition of its status as an

OSS legacy agency. Multiple members of OSS found a home at DIA after its dissolution, including Capt. Ottis Stephenson, Lt. Gen. William Quinn and Lt. Gen. Samuel Wilson, who served as DIA's first deputy comptroller, first deputy director and fifth director, respectively.

The medal features the inscription OSS with a paratrooper and two civilians, a man and a woman, which represents the broad range of efforts undertaken by the OSS. Each is rendered as a shape without details, hinting at the way agents sought to operate anonymously. The dates 1942-1945 are to recognizing the years in which the OSS operated. The reverse of the medal features the OSS spearhead inscribed with code words related to important OSS missions and agents.

The OSS was the first organized effort by the United States to implement a centralized system of strategic intelligence. It is the predecessor to CIA, the U.S. Special Operations Command, U.S. Special Forces and the U.S. Department of State's Bureau of Intelligence and Research.

The OSS Congressional Gold Medal Act was signed into law on December 14, 2016, and was presented at a ceremony on Capitol Hill. It led another successful effort to have the OSS and original CIA headquarters on Navy Hill in Washington, D.C., added to the National Register of Historic Places.

After remarks on his connection to the OSS and their sacrificial bravery during the Dawes mission in 1944, former DIA director and OSS Society representative, retired Lt. Gen. Patrick Hughes, presented the OSS Congressional Gold Medal to the current DIA director, Lt. Gen. Robert P. Ashley Jr.

Upon receiving the award, Ashley reaffirmed the relationship between the OSS and DIA by reading an excerpt from OSS founder Maj. Gen. William Donovan's

"Memorandum of Establishment of Service of Strategic Information."

"The basic purpose of this (agency) is to constitute a means by which the President, as Commander-in-Chief, and his strategic Board would have available accurate and complete enemy intelligence reports upon which military operational decisions could be based," Ashley said.

Ashley then gave special thanks to the guest of honor, retired Maj. James Thompson, for his service in the OSS, noting the impact OSS had on him as a young lieutenant.

"These are the stories that brought us into this field, the sense of adventure, mystique, the feeling that you could do something amazing for your nation," he said.

Ashley closed by responding to an earlier comment from Thompson on how the OSS was filled with people who had Ph.D.s, but could hold their own in a fight.

"That is a rare breed," Ashley said with a smile. "But we still do have some of those. Mr. Thompson. Rest assured, this generation is up to the task."

Heroic clandestine warriors of the OSS finally get Congressional Gold Medal after 70 year wait

By <u>Jennifer Harper</u> - *The Washington Times - Thursday, December 1, 2016*

The innovative clandestine warriors of the World War II era have finally earned their well-deserved recognition after a wait which spanned seven decades.

The Office of Strategic Services Congressional Gold Medal Act was passed Wednesday by the U.S. House of Representatives, a final chapter in the push to honor members of the "OSS" — the forerunner to both the CIA and the U.S. special operations forces. The Senate unanimously passed the bipartisan legislation earlier this year.

"For many years, the heroic contributions of the OSS — which included some of the most daring covert operations of World War II — remained shrouded in secrecy, their contributions largely unknown to the American public," said Sen. Mark Warner, Virginia Democrat, who cosponsored the Senate bill with Sen. Roy Blunt, Missouri Republican. "Today, Congress is able to publicly recognize the members of the OSS for their remarkable heroism and many sacrifices.

"The OSS once boasted nearly 13,000 members, but more than 70 years after they won the war, fewer than 100 are still with us," Mr. Warner added. "I know how much it means to the veterans of the OSS, as well as their families, that this legislation is finally making its way to the President's desk to be signed into law."

The roster of OSS personnel includes distinguished and famous names such as Hollywood actors Marlene Dietrich and Sterling Hayden; Fred Mayer, the real "inglorious bastard" who was nominated for the Medal of Honor; celebrity chef Julia Child, Nobel Peace Prize winner Ralph Bunche, film director John Ford, Pulitzer Prize recipient Arthur Schlesinger Jr. and four CIA directors — William Casey, William Colby, Allen Dulles and Richard Helms.

The OSS itself was shepherded into action in 1942 by Army Maj. Gen. William J. Donovan. The force grappled with "silent, unending work of keeping America safe" against Nazis and other American enemies and became known for their bold, often creative methods of warfare.

"The Office of Strategic Services was filled with patriots who honorably served their country while making an enormous contribution to the defeat of the Axis powers,"

H. R. 3929

To award the Congressional Gold Medal, collectively, to the members of the Office of Strategic Services (OSS) in recognition of their superior service and major contributions during World War II.

IN THE HOUSE OF REPRESENTATIVES

NOVEMBER 4, 2015

Mr. LATTA (for himself, Mr. FRANKS of Arizona, Mr. PITTENGER, Mr. STEWART, Mr. JONES, Mr. PETERS, Mr. MCKINLEY, Mr. SCHWEIKERT, Mr. HUNTER, Mr. TURNER, Mr. KING of New York, Mr.MEEKS, Mr. MILLER of Florida, Mr. CARSON of Indiana, Mr. VAN HOLLEN, Mr. THOMPSON of Pennsylvania, Mr. KING of Iowa, Mr. RUSSELL, Mr. GIBBS, Ms. KAPTUR, Mr. FORBES, Miss Rice of New York, Mr. HIGGINS, Mr. JOLLY, Mr. MESSER, Mr. WALBERG, Mr. LARSON of Connecticut, Mrs. COMSTOCK, Mr. DESANTIS, and Mr. ZINKE) introduced the following bill; which was referred to the Committee on Financial Services, and in addition to the Committee on House Administration, for a period to be subsequently determined by the Speaker, in each case for consideration of such provisions as fall within the jurisdiction of the committee concerned

---

A BILL

To award the Congressional Gold Medal, collectively, to the members of the Office of Strategic Services (OSS) in recognition of their superior service and major contributions during World War II.

Be it enacted by the Senate and House of Representatives of the United States of America in Congress assembled,

SECTION 1. SHORT TITLE.

This Act may be cited as the "Office of Strategic Services Congressional Gold Medal Act".

SEC. 2. FINDINGS.

The Congress finds the following:

(1) The Office of Strategic Services (OSS) was America's first effort to implement a system of strategic intelligence during World War II and provided the basis for the modern-day American intelligence and special operations communities. The U.S. Special Operations Command and the National Clandestine Service chose the OSS spearhead as their insignias.

(2) OSS founder General William J. Donovan is the only person in American history to receive our Nation's four highest decorations, including the Medal of Honor. Upon learning of his death in 1959, President Eisenhower called General Donovan the "last hero". In addition to founding and leading the OSS, General Donovan was also selected by President Roosevelt, who called him his "secret legs", as an emissary to Great Britain and continental Europe before the United States entered World War II.

(3) All the military branches during World War II contributed personnel to the OSS. The present-day Special Operations Forces trace their lineage to the OSS. Its Maritime Unit was a precursor to the U.S. Navy SEALs. The OSS Operational Groups and Jedburghs were forerunners to U.S. Army Special Forces. The 801st/492nd Bombardment Group ("Carpetbaggers") were progenitors to the Air Force Special Operations Command. The Marines who served in the OSS, including the actor Sterling Hayden (a Silver Star recipient), Col. William Eddy (a Distinguished Service Cross recipient who was described as the "nearest thing the United States has had to a Lawrence of Arabia"), and Col. Peter Ortiz (a two-time Navy Cross recipient), were predecessors to the Marine Special Operations Command. U.S. Coast Guard personnel were recruited for the Maritime Unit and its Operational Swimmer Group.

(4) The OSS organized, trained, supplied, and fought with resistance organizations throughout Europe and Asia that played an important role in America's victory during World War II. General Eisenhower credited the OSS's covert contribution in France to the equivalent to having an extra military division. General Eisenhower told General Donovan that if it did nothing else, the

photographic reconnaissance conducted by the OSS prior to the D-Day Invasion justified its creation.

(5) Four future directors of central intelligence served as OSS officers: William Casey, William Colby, Allen Dulles, and Richard Helms.

(6) Women comprised more than one-third of OSS personnel and played a critical role in the organization. They included Virginia Hall, the only civilian female to receive a Distinguished Service Cross in World War II, and Julia Child.

(7) OSS recruited Fritz Kolbe, a German diplomat who became America's most important spy against the Nazis in World War II.

(8) America's leading scientists and scholars served in the OSS Research and Analysis Branch, including Ralph Bunche, the first African-American to receive the Nobel Peace Prize; Pulitzer Prize-winning historian Arthur Schlesinger, Jr.; Supreme Court Justice Arthur Goldberg; Sherman Kent; John King Fairbank; and Walt Rostow. Its ranks included seven future presidents of the American Historical Association, five of the American Economic Association, and two Nobel laureates.

(9) The U.S. Department of State's Bureau of Intelligence and Research traces its creation to the OSS Research and Analysis Branch.

(10) James Donovan, who was portrayed by Tom Hanks in the Steven Spielberg movie "Bridge of Spies" and negotiated the release of U–2 pilot Francis Gary Powers, served as General Counsel of the OSS.

(11) The OSS invented and employed new technology through its Research and Development Branch, inventing new weapons and revolutionary communications equipment. Dr. Christian Lambertsen invented the first underwater rebreathing apparatus that was first utilized by the OSS and is known today as SCUBA.

(12) OSS Detachment 101 operated in Burma and pioneered the art of unconventional warfare. It was the first United States unit to deploy a large guerrilla army deep in enemy territory. It has been credited with the highest kill/loss ratio for any infantry-type unit in American military history and was awarded a Presidential Unit Citation.

(13) Its X–2 branch pioneered counterintelligence with the British and established the modern counterintelligence community. The network of contacts built by the OSS with foreign intelligence services led to enduring Cold War alliances.

(14) Operation Torch, the Allied invasion of French North Africa in November 1942, was aided by the networks established and information acquired by the OSS to guide Allied landings.

(15) OSS Operation Halyard rescued more than 500 downed airmen trapped behind enemy lines in Yugoslavia, one of the most daring and successful rescue operations of World War II.

(16) OSS "Mercy Missions" at the end of World War II saved the lives of thousands of Allied prisoners of war whom it was feared would be murdered by the Japanese.

(17) The handful of surviving men and women of the OSS whom General Donovan said performed "some of the bravest acts of the war" are members of the "Greatest Generation". They have never been collectively recognized for their heroic and pioneering service in World War II.

SEC. 3. CONGRESSIONAL GOLD MEDAL.

(a) PRESENTATION AUTHORIZED.—The Speaker of the House of Representatives and the President pro tempore of the Senate shall make appropriate arrangements for the presentation, on behalf of the Congress, of a gold medal of appropriate design in commemoration to the members of the Office of Strategic Services (OSS), in recognition of their superior service and major contributions during World War II.

(b) DESIGN AND STRIKING.—For purposes of the presentation referred to in subsection (a), the Secretary of the Treasury (referred to in this Act as the "Secretary") shall strike a gold medal with suitable emblems, devices, and inscriptions, to be determined by the Secretary.

(c) SMITHSONIAN INSTITUTION.—

(1) IN GENERAL.—Following the award of the gold medal in commemoration to the members of the Office of Strategic Services under subsection (a), the gold medal shall be given to the Smithsonian Institution, where it will be displayed as appropriate and made available for research.

(2) SENSE OF CONGRESS.—It is the sense of Congress that the Smithsonian Institution should make the gold medal received under paragraph (1) available for display elsewhere, particularly at other appropriate locations associated with the Office of Strategic Services.

SEC. 4. DUPLICATE MEDALS.

The Secretary may strike and sell duplicates in bronze of the gold medal struck pursuant to section 3 under such regulations as the Secretary may prescribe, at a price sufficient to cover the cost thereof, including labor, materials, dies, use of machinery, and overhead expenses, and the cost of the gold medal.

SEC. 5. STATUS OF MEDALS.

(a) NATIONAL MEDALS.—The medals struck pursuant to this Act are national medals for purposes of chapter 51 of title 31, United States Code.

(b) NUMISMATIC ITEMS.—For purposes of section 5134 of title 31, United States Code, all medals struck under this Act shall be considered to be numismatic items.

The Office of Strategic Services Society

The Office of Strategic Services (OSS) Society honors the historic accomplishments of the OSS during World War II, the first organized effort by the United States to implement a centralized system of strategic intelligence and the predecessor to the Central Intelligence Agency, the U.S. Special Operations Command, U.S. Special Forces, and the U.S. Department of State's Bureau of Intelligence and Research. It educates the American public regarding the continuing importance of strategic intelligence and special operations to the preservation of freedom. The OSS Society was founded in 1947 by General William Donovan as the Veterans of OSS. It was based in New York City for 50 years. In 1997, it became The OSS Society and moved to Washington, D.C.

The OSS Society led a successful effort to have a Congressional Gold Medal awarded to the OSS. The OSS Congressional Gold Medal Act was signed into law on December 14, 2016, and was presented at a ceremony on Capitol Hill. It led another successful effort to have the OSS and original CIA headquarters on Navy Hill in Washington, D.C., added to the National Register of Historic Places. It hosts the William J. Donovan Award® Dinner, the preeminent annual gathering of the US intelligence and special operations communities. The OSS Society has established OSS memorials throughout the United States and in Europe. It publishes *The OSS Society Journal*. The OSS Society is planning to build the National Museum of Intelligence and Special Operations® that will honor Americans who have served at the "tip of the spear" and inspire future generations to serve their country.

The OSS Society is a 501(c)(3) charitable organization. All donations are tax deductible to the fullest extent of the law. Membership in The OSS Society is available to OSS veterans, their descendants, current and former members of the U.S. intelligence, national security, and special operations communities, and people who are interested in General Donovan's "unusual experiment" - the Office of Strategic Services.

The OSS Society:
Keepers of Gen. Donovan's Flame

By Susan L. Kerr and John D. Gresham

"We were not afraid to make mistakes because we were not afraid to try things that had not been tried before." "You can't succeed without taking chances."
– Maj. Gen. William J. Donovan, OSS founder

"I'm responsible for a group of very dangerous senior citizens."
– Charles Pinck, president of the OSS Society

Ask any American adult about the CIA and there's a good chance he'll be able to identify its basic intelligence gathering functions. Ask the same person about military special operations and he'll probably be able to speak somewhat about the Green Berets in Afghanistan and Iraq. Ask him what he knows about World War II's Office of Strategic Services (OSS) and he'll likely stare blankly at the question. Such is the state of public knowledge about America's first central intelligence agency. The Office of Strategic Services was the first organized American intelligence initiative, conceived and put into action on June

13, 1942, by President Franklin D. Roosevelt on the advice of the top British intelligence officer in the Western Hemisphere, William Stephenson (known as "the man called "Intrepid") and William J. Donovan, a World War I hero, leading attorney, and an informal advisor to the president. Prior to that time, intelligence gathering was achieved on a piecemeal fashion. With the commencement of hostilities and the surprise attack on Pearl Harbor, the need for a central intelligence office to amass information, analyze it, and make recommendations for appropriate action became clear overnight. During its brief lifetime, just a few months short of four years, the OSS overshot these goals, setting the stage for the creation of both the Central Intelligence Agency and the U.S. special operations forces (SOFs). Eschewing the limelight, its recruits performed amazing feats of derring-do befitting the movies, and counted among its operatives several Hollywood figures such as swashbuckling actor Douglas Fairbanks Jr., Academy Award-winning director John Ford, and Sterling Hayden, who won a Silver Star for bravery behind enemy lines. The majority were above-average Joes, and some Josephines, recruited from the ranks of the U.S. military, along with civilian trades and well-traveled intellectuals. An ideal OSS candidate was once described as a "Ph.D. who can win a bar fight" and Donovan described OSS personnel as his "glorious amateurs." The man who assembled this stellar cast was perhaps the biggest and quietest swashbuckler of them all: Medal of Honor recipient Gen. William "Wild Bill" Donovan. Donovan was one of those larger-than life characters who strides across the landscape of history when he is needed most. He had been performing ad-hoc intelligence work well before Dec. 7, 1941. Roosevelt called Donovan his "secret legs." Since that time, military and intelligence professionals have appreciated and admired Donovan's depth of perception and breadth of vision. Richard

Helms, director of central intelligence (DCI) from 1966 to 1973 and an OSS alumnus, said: "He was truly the father of American intelligence. Before him, our efforts were trivial." Donovan's personal qualities became the recruiting criteria for the infant OSS: a potent combination of brains, brawn, and bravado. Recruits were encouraged to improvise and innovate. Donovan placed a high value on initiative and courage, saying that he would "rather have a young lieutenant with enough guts to disobey a direct order than a colonel too regimented to think and act for himself." He encouraged risk-taking or, as he called it, "calculated recklessness." He backed up his people when they stumbled. However, these unorthodox principles didn't win friends within the regular military and government circles. William J. Casey, one of Donovan's OSS recruits and DCI from 1981 to 1987 remembered, "You didn't wait six months for a feasibility study to prove that an idea could work. You gambled that it might work. You didn't tie up the organization with red tape designed mostly to cover somebody's butt. You took the initiative and the responsibility. You went around end; you went over somebody's head if you had to. But you acted. That's what drove the regular military and the State Department chair-warmers crazy about the OSS." This is the part of Donovan's legacy that lives on in the special operations community. Two units within OSS, the Jedburghs and operational groups, forerunners of today's U.S. SOF, parachuted into Europe and Asia behind enemy lines to work with resistance groups. They had to become instantaneous peacekeepers and diplomats when dealing with partisan bands bent on revenge against certain elements of their own countrymen, improvising all the way. Nearly anyone can be trained to be a killer. Only the very best can synthesize the attributes of citizen, soldier, spy, and diplomat into one remarkable human being. War does not last forever, and in April 1945, Donovan's strongest supporter,

Roosevelt, died. The succession of President Harry S. Truman to the presidency meant trouble for Donovan and the OSS. It was a clash of personalities and wills from the start. Donovan's iconoclastic leadership style simply did not mesh with the organizational-man mindset of Truman, who knew little about intelligence gathering. FBI Director J. Edgar Hoover, a longtime Donovan and OSS nemesis, drew out his long knives. With his signing of an Executive Order on Sept. 20, 1945, the Office of Strategic Services was no more, its activities split up between the Department of War and the Department of State. Just two years later, however, the need for one main intelligence organization became apparent as the Soviet Union emerged from World War II bent on surpassing its former allies. Passage of the National Security Act in 1947 found the Truman administration creating a new clandestine agency to replace the defunct Office of Strategic Services, the Central Intelligence Agency, using a plan created by Donovan. Most of its early members were OSS alumni. But most demobilized OSS personnel scattered across the county, either picking up professions interrupted by the war, advancing in rank within the military, or committing themselves to lives as public servants. Donovan himself returned to the practice of law for a time, serving as special assistant to Telford Taylor, the chief prosecutor of Nazi war criminals at the Nuremberg War Crime Tribunals. After obtaining justice for OSS personnel killed, sometimes gruesomely, by the Germans, he went back to his highly successful Wall Street law firm while still offering his unique experience and insight to American presidents, eventually serving as ambassador to Thailand for a year under President Dwight D. Eisenhower. Upon learning of Donovan's death in 1959, Eisenhower said: "What a man! We have lost the last hero." Other OSS graduates continued careers in the intelligence community. Allen Dulles, William Colby, Helms, and Casey went on to lead the CIA. To a man, each credited Donovan for setting worthy goals and core values for their community. Gen. John Singlaub, who was a member of the Jedburghs, remained in the military and left an indelible mark on what was to become the U.S. Army Special Forces, the Navy SEALs, and other SOF communities among the service branches. The men and women of the Office of Strategic Services shared a brief and unique experience under Donovan's tutelage. Unable to truly share their tales and life-changing experiences with others who served in World War II, it was perhaps only natural that they would stay together after the war. Thus, the Veterans of Strategic Services (VOSS) was born in 1947 as a means of keeping the organization's spirit alive. Estimates of the number of OSS members during the war are in the range of 13,000. Of these, perhaps 1,000 to 1,500 participated in the activities of the VOSS at its peak. Initially social in nature, VOSS evolved over time to preserve its unique history and to honor those who followed in Donovan's footsteps. The first William J. Donovan Award®, which honors the outstanding attributes of the OSS's founder who had passed away in 1959, was presented to Dulles in 1961. Other recipients have included Prime Minister Margaret Thatcher, President Ronald Reagan, Lord Mountbatten, Sir William Stephenson, Gen. David Petraeus, and Maj. Gen. John Singlaub. In the late 1990s, as its members were aging and concerned that the contributions of Donovan and his OSS might be forgotten over time; VOSS changed its name to The OSS Society and moved its headquarters from Rockefeller Center in New York City to Washington, D.C. The son of one of the VOSS members, Charles Pinck, urged his father, Dan Pinck, who served behind enemy lines in China, to attend one of the last big gatherings of OSS veterans in the mid-1980s, an event populated with people like Casey, Colby, and Helms. Intrigued and inspired by his father's OSS service, Pinck volunteered to help VOSS when he moved to Washington in the early 1990s and became president of The OSS Society in 2002. Today, Charles Pinck is a man on a mission to keep the memory of OSS alive, and to apply lessons learned by the OSS in World War II to present-day challenges. The OSS Society recently held a symposium, for example, with the Joint Special Operations University ("Irregular Warfare and the OSS Model") that is available online at www.ossreborn.com. The OSS Society is no longer limited to OSS veterans. Its members include descendants of OSS veterans, current and retired members of the U.S. intelligence community and U.S. special operations forces, academics, and others with a serious interest in the OSS. Its board of directors includes Adm. Eric Olson, Gen. Bryan Brown, President George H.W. Bush, and five former directors of central intelligence. In addition to presenting the William J. Donovan Award, The OSS Society also bestows its Distinguished Service Award. Usually reserved for OSS veterans, there have been notable exceptions, such as its presentation to an Eastern European partisan, Maria Gulovich, who saved the lives of an OSS team in Slovakia. In 1946, Donovan personally awarded Gulovich the Bronze Star at West Point in front of the Corps of Cadets, the first woman so honored. In 2009, the recipient was Dr. Christian Lambertson, Ph.D., who was instrumental in the development of combat rebreather systems for the OSS and post-war SOF organizations. The OSS Society publishes The OSS Society Journal, offers research assistance and speakers upon request, hosts an online discussion group with more than 1,200 members, and has erected OSS memorials throughout the United States. Pinck's major goal is the creation of an OSS museum in the Washington, D.C.-metro area. "This wouldn't be just an archive or a library, but a fully interactive museum that would tell the remarkable story of Gen. Donovan and OSS and the contributions made to it by all our military services. Too few Americans know about the

OSS: The most remarkable organization ever created by the U.S. government." But at its core, the OSS Society will always be about the values and achievements of the OSS and its founder, Gen. William Donovan. For in the middle of the greatest conflict in the history of the world, for a few years, it was OSS that put forward America's best, brightest, and bravest. To learn more about The OSS Society, please visit its Web site at www.osssociety.org.

Reprinted from The New York Times
When the Rounds Were Ammo

By BILL PENNINGTON JUNE 12, 2011

The soldiers arrived in the dead of night, packed shoulder to shoulder in trucks with canvas walls that obscured the route to a secret destination. They were the first World War II recruits for a new covert operation called the Office of Strategic Services, a long, vague name that hid what the soldiers would become: spies, saboteurs, commandos and undercover agents.

The troops were unloaded at a large, bland tent city.

"It was six of us to a tent with a potbelly stove in the middle," said the O.S.S. veteran Caesar Civitella, describing the night in 1943. "We had been sworn to complete secrecy. They told us to go to sleep, so we went to sleep."

When the soldiers emerged from their tents in the morning, they turned to glimpse a palace beside the campsite, an immense Mediterranean-inspired clubhouse overlooking a Shangri-La — the rolling hills and golf holes of Congressional Country Club, site of this week's 111th United States Open.

During World War II, the club's more than 400 acres about 12 miles outside Washington had been leased to the United States government to serve as the training ground for America's first intelligence agency, the forerunner to the C.I.A. and American Special Forces.

"We came out of the tent and thought, 'Hey, country club living,' " Civitella said.

"But we were wrong; it was no country club life." In fact, another O.S.S. veteran, Alex MacDonald, later called the training at Congressional "malice in wonderland."

The practice range became a rifle range, and bunkers were used for grenade practice. The dense wooded areas were perfect for nighttime commando exercises, and an obstacle course, set with booby traps, stretched across the first and second holes. Hand-to-hand combat was taught next to a mock fuselage from which paratroopers learned to jump. Men crawled on their bellies across fairways sprayed with live machine gun fire, and the greens made excellent targets for mortar practice. So did the caddie shack and every rain shelter on the course. "We literally just blew the place up," said Al Johnson, who, like most of the living O.S.S. veterans — there are about 200 — is in his late 80s.

When the world's best golfers play Congressional this week in Bethesda, Md., little evidence of the mayhem that preceded them by more than 65 years will remain. After the war, the federal government restored the course to its original splendor. Golf shots replaced gunshots.

"But Congressional remains a pivotal place in the history of the country," Charles Pinck, president of the O.S.S. Society, said. "It's the birthplace of the American Special Forces. And groups like the Navy Seals — the Congressional Country Club is where it all started."

The 18th hole and the clubhouse at Congressional Country Club, where more than 2,500 soldiers passed through from 1943 to 1945. Credit Nick Wass/Associated Press

It was an eclectic collection of fighting men who arrived at Congressional in 1943. Most were drawn from the United States military, pulled aside because of one aptitude or another, like familiarity with a foreign language. They would be asked if they wanted to volunteer for hazardous duty and would face physical and psychological testing to determine if they could handle life behind enemy lines. Founded by the World War I hero William Donovan, who was known as Wild Bill, the O.S.S. recruited from civilian trades and sought well-traveled intellectuals as well. An ideal O.S.S. candidate was once described as a "Ph.D. who can win a bar fight."

The troops at Congressional, known to them as Area F, were generally trained in groups of about 200 men. From 1943 to 1945, more than 2,500 soldiers passed through Congressional. The officers lived in the clubhouse, where the grand ballroom was turned into a classroom and the dining room was a mess hall. They did little marching or traditional, regimented military drilling.

"The idea was not to build discipline but innovation," said John Whiteclay Chambers II, a history professor at Rutgers University who has written extensively about the O.S.S. training. "They wanted to create men who would be daring, aggressive and imaginative. They had them work together to build a stone bridge over a creek on the golf course. Then they would ask them what's the best way to demolish it, using plastic explosives?"

Nighttime brought the grounds alive with missions not unlike the child's game capture the flag, except the sentries were armed and the commandos carried scalpel-sharp stilettos. Pity the poor milkman assigned to make deliveries to Congressional; he was the target of more than one ambush.

Of his time at Congressional, MacDonald once said, "It was the 10 Commandments in reverse: lie and steal, kill, maim, spy."

Andrew Mousalimas, another O.S.S. veteran, said: "There was nothing ordinary about our training because there was nothing ordinary about what they were asking us to do in battle. We might have to operate completely by ourselves behind enemy lines. We had to be ready for anything."

Three O.S.S. recruits died during the exercises at Congressional, Chambers said.

Congressional had a long relationship with Washington's elite, going back to 1923, when Herbert Hoover, then the Secretary of Commerce, helped lay the cornerstone of the clubhouse. Presidents, cabinet members, generals and admirals had been members. But Prohibition and the Depression had been hard on the club's finances. The $4,000 annual rent the government paid during the war — along with the restoration efforts — may have saved Congressional.

If the O.S.S. trainees felt the juxtaposition of training for the drudgery and strain of combat in a place of great privilege, they did not dwell on it.

"Maybe 10 percent of us had ever played golf, so we didn't even know about that world," said Johnson, who served in North Africa, France and China. "We made a joke or two about going to tee off, but we were pretty focused on where we were headed and what we needed to learn to be ready."

The O.S.S. veterans have returned to Congressional for several reunions.

"I have to remind them not to blow anything up," said Pinck of the O.S.S. Society, which includes descendants of veterans and members of the American intelligence and Special Forces community. Pinck's father, Dan, served as an operative behind enemy lines in China.

The reunions have allowed the veterans to discuss their service, which they generally had not done since World War II. During the war, O.S.S. members were instructed never to discuss their missions or their training, even with relatives. When the war ended, a similar silence about their role continued, for as long as 50 years. It was said that O.S.S. stood for "Oh So Secret."

"Getting together was great for letting all the stories out," Johnson said. "Sometimes it was like we were all back at Area F."

Johnson said that he had become a semi-regular golfer in retirement and that he would watch the 2011 United States Open. He said the world's golfing elite would have a far easier time navigating the Congressional course this week than they would have in 1943.

"Back then, it would have been hard just finding the greens," Johnson said with a laugh. "And we left some divots that no golfer could have gotten out of in less than three shots."

West Michigan WWII spy says Congressional Gold Medal was 'long overdue'

Posted Mar 26, 2018
By Bryce Airgood | bairgood@mlive.com

GRAND RAPIDS, MI - Hudsonville resident and World War II veteran Elsworth "Al" Johnson, 94, said receiving the Congressional Gold Medal last week was "long overdue."

Johnson and other remaining members of the Office of Strategic Services, including another Hudsonville man, were honored Wednesday, March 21, in Washington, D.C.

More than 70 years after the end of World War II, the group received the Congressional Gold Medal, the highest civilian honor bestowed by Congress.

The Office of Strategic Services was the forerunner of the CIA and, during the war, called upon the U.S. Army Air Forces to conduct special operations based from the United Kingdom, according to the National Museum of the U.S. Air Force website.

Johnson said he was a spy for the Office of Strategic Services during World War II.

His team specifically parachuted behind enemy lines in France and later China. Its job was to collect information about enemy forces.

Founded by General William J. Donovan, a Medal of Honor recipient, the Office of Strategic Services organized, trained, supplied and fought in the war throughout Europe and Asia and played a decisive role in the United States' victory over Axis forces, according to a news release from U.S. House Speaker Paul Ryan's office.

Johnson said the organization was the predecessor to the Special Forces and the father of all things covert and subversive.

After the war ended, members were not allowed to speak to anyone about their experiences.

"We were a silent organization. Nobody knew who we were," Johnson said in a previous MLive interview.

The release of documents on the 50th anniversary of the war's end in 1995 freed him to finally share his memories.

Johnson detailed his experiences in a memoir titled "One Small Part."

Nancy Moseler, Johnson's daughter, said she was glad they were finally able to honor her father and the other service members, especially since they needed to be quiet for so long.

Johnson joined the service at the "strapping" age of 18, he said, when he felt like he could conquer the world and was too young to be afraid. He served for three years, from 1943 to 1945, and worked behind enemy lines doing the grunt work, he said.

"We were the ones who did the dirty work," Johnson said.

One of Johnson's missions was in July 1945, where Office of Strategic Services troops parachuted into the rice paddies of central China. It was their job to disrupt the supply of rice back to Japan.

"I never thought we would live through the Chinese operation because we were so easily identified," Johnson said in a previous MLive interview.

They were sent as "advisers," Johnson said, their orders prohibiting them from taking part in combat.

Their role was further complicated by a growing civil war between nationalist forces and communist forces led by Mao Tse-tung.

"We carried a lot of Chinese money with us. You bought intelligence. You bought loyalty," he said.

The war ended with the Japanese surrender on Aug. 15, 1945, and Johnson was finally home by the end of the year. He said they did not have humorous adventures during the war, as they were often being shot at and shooting other people.

"That was serious," Johnson said.

His daughter and son went with him to Washington, D.C., for the ceremony. He said he thinks they are proud.

"And I'm proud of them for being patient with an old man," Johnson

Fox 17 TV:

HUDSONVILLE, Mich. -- An American treasure, WWII veteran Al Johnson transformed his home office in Hudsonville into memories from 73 years ago Thursday: he wore his English beret as he carefully reviewed his documents and pictures.

On March 21, 2017 Johnson, now 94, will be in Washington DC alongside surviving members of the Office of Strategic Services to receive the Congressional Gold Medal, the highest civilian honor in the nation. He served in the OSS from 1943 to 1945. The OSS is the predecessor of both Special Forces and the CIA.

"Office of Strategic Service: It was a spy, sabotage organization, saboteurs and counter espionage, anything that was subversive we fell in that category," said Johnson with FOX 17 Thursday, a jokester who's sharp.

Initially drafted at 19 and then trained as a surgical nurse, Johnson says he volunteered for the OSS the moment he read their flier.

"I was a strapping 19-year-old," said Johnson, "Felt like I could conquer the world."

"I wanted to get into the fight; I didn't want to see the results of the fight," he laughed. "When you're 19, what are you going to walk around being a bedpan jockey your whole life? Forget it. I wanted some action."

Using a golf club, he pinpointed to FOX 17 on a preserved silk map of central France, exactly where he parachuted from only 500 feet off the ground from a bomber model he hung from his office ceiling.

Johnson says he and his OSS team attacked and preserved key infrastructure in several countries, showing a picture from June of 1944 of his 18-person group, which used the code name "Patrick."

After France, with several missions in between, Johnson volunteered to continue to serve in China, where his OSS team went by the name "Blueberry." There he recalled staying put for nearly a month after the war ended, as Japanese forces fought on.

"There's the Blueberry group," he said pointing to their picture. "I found my thrill on Blueberry Hill, on Blueberry Hill, when I met you," he sang with a smile.

Sharing his first-hand accounts of the peril he and his fellow OSS members faced, these are all memories he kept to himself for decades until his service became declassified in 1995. That's the year Johnson wrote his unpublished book, "One Small Part."

"It wasn't for 50 years, so I had to keep my mouth shut, which I thought was bad because I couldn't even tell my parents," Johnson said, sharing his father served in WWI.

Legends of incredible stories and courage Johnson can finally tell, and share a laugh or two about.

WWII veteran and Congressional Medal recipient welcomed home by patriot guard

Author: Jaleesa Irizarry
Published: 4:27 PM EDT March 22, 2018
Updated: 6:43 PM EDT March 22, 2018
Wzzm13.com -13 On your Side

Al Johnson is having a week.

After he received a Congressional Gold Medal, the 94-year-old was greeted back to West Michigan with a hero's welcome.

The Patriot Guard riders lined Concourse B at Gerald R. Ford airport with American flags in hand. The group was waiting for Johnson to come home from Washington D.C.

"I think it's important because today's people have started to look other ways. I think it's special that we've been given the honor and the privilege to be able to do it and without the people out there doing this? They're fighting the wars," Dani Jennings, Captain of the area Patriot Guard, said.

Al Johnson was wheeled through the line of riders by his son, Jim. Once he got to the end, the first person he looked for was his wife of 70 years, Jean.

"Give me a kiss babe," he said as he leaned toward the 97-year-old.

Many of Johnson's relatives and friends also greeted him and a few flyers stopped to take the moment in.

"I didn't know I had so many friends," he said as everyone belted in laughter.

Johnson never thought he'd get this kind of treatment. The Hudsonville man was part of the Office of Strategic Services during the war, the predecessor of the CIA. Much of the information of who was in the OSS was classified until 2008.

"Well I almost broke down in tears," Johnson said as he reacted to the Patriot Guard's welcome. "The organization was secret so no one knew anything about it so they couldn't honor you in any way."

But that all changed Thursday afternoon as he clutched on to his heavy gold medal and was wheeled out of the airport. After a week of honor, recognition, and pride, there's only one thing left to do.

"Probably sleep for a week," he said.

Posted Apr 10, 2018 Holland Sentinel By Jake Allen

Seventy three years later, Al Johnson was recognized in Washington D.C. for his service with the OSS during WWII.

Al Johnson, a 94-year-old World War II veteran from Hudsonville, said it's hard for people to remember something that never existed from the perspective of the general public.

Johnson served in the Office of Strategic Services during WWII, which was the predecessor to the CIA and was a secret organization that those involved with could not talk about even after returning home from the war.

Seventy-three years after the war, Johnson was recognized in Washington, D.C., for his service with the OSS.

He and about 23 other members of the OSS were awarded the Congressional Gold Medal on March 21.

"It was a non-glorious organization," Johnson said. "We couldn't receive glory because we didn't exist, which is hard to believe."

For years, Johnson had to tell his friends and family he was a paratrooper in WWII and couldn't talk about his time serving in the OSS because of the secrecy of the organization. He said the recognition was long overdue.

Johnson brought his son Jim Johnson, 64, and daughter Nancy Moseler, 67, with him to Washington, D.C., to receive the award. After the ceremony, Johnson was congratulated by U.S. Rep. Bill Huizenga, R-Zeeland.

"Members of the OSS did a lot to contribute during WWII and they wanted to tell their stories," Moseler said. "They were never appreciated. Now they are able to tell some of those stories and it's important they get the most recognition possible."

At its peak, the OSS had about 13,000 men and women in the organization, according to **cia.gov**. The OSS was America's first strategic intelligence system and was implemented during World War II.

It is widely considered the foundation of modern day intelligence operations, according to a news release from U.S. House Speaker Paul Ryan's office regarding the Congressional Gold Medal ceremony.

The medal is the highest civilian honor the United States can bestow. In accordance with Public Law 114–269, a single gold medal was struck to collectively honor the members of the OSS, including Johnson.

Johnson graduated high school in Grand Rapids in 1942 and was drafted into the war in 1943.

As an 18-year-old, Johnson was assigned to the medical corps in the U.S. Army.

"I took surgical nurse training," Johnson said. "I hated it. I didn't want to be some bedpan jockey."

After a notice looking for volunteers for "hazardous duty with a short life expectancy" was posted, Johnson immediately signed up to volunteer. This was when his involvement with the OSS began.

"There was no fighting down at the medical corp," Johnson said. "I wanted to do the fighting. I was 18 and I thought I could conquer the world."

Johnson was interviewed by psychiatrists and officers from the OSS to see if he qualified for the program.

"They needed men who could psychologically live behind enemy lines for an extended period of time," Johnson said. "Not everybody can do that and a lot of people fall apart right away."

After being accepted into the program and months of training, Johnson parachuted into southern France on Aug. 12, 1944.

"Our mission was to capture a hydroelectric plant and hold it for the southern invasion of troops to come up," Johnson said.

After capturing the plant, Johnson and his fellow OSS members spent their time ambushing German troops.

"We did anything to disrupt the enemy," Johnson said. "It was more of a psychological war as much as a physical war. They didn't know where we were going to hit next."

Johnson was stationed in France for about six weeks until the Allied Forces' invasion caught up. Then he was given the option to return to the regular Army or continue serving with the OSS — he chose the OSS.

His next mission was in China.

In 1945, Johnson parachuted in with the mission of disrupting the flow of rice from China to Japan.

"China was a more difficult mission because we were so un-Chinese," Johnson said. "You could tell because we didn't look like the Chinese, so it was hard to blend in."

After several months in China, U.S. forces dropped atomic bombs on two Japanese cities and the war would end soon after.

"The radio message came across and it said we couldn't leave China yet because all of the Japanese had not surrendered yet."

Johnson's war ended about 30 days after the official end of WWII, he said.

After working their way through China, Johnson and fellow OSS members flew out and arrived home at the end of 1945.

"All the hoopla was done already," Johnson said. "No one cared whether we came or went. We received no hoopla, no parades, no decorations, no nothing."

The Congressional Gold Medal was needed recognition for this and a lot of other reasons, Johnson said.

"We were happy to get the Congressional Gold Medal because it was recognition that was overdue," Johnson said. "The OSS, being a secret organization, was ignored in many of the write-ups and conversations regarding the war."

Hudsonville veteran recalls secret missions for CIA's predecessor in World War II

Posted May 31, 2011
By Ted Roelofs | The Grand Rapids Press

Years before the CIA formed, decades before the spy agency helped hunt down Osama bin Laden, there was something called the Office of Strategic Services.

Georgetown Township resident Al Johnson could tell you a tale or two about that.

Johnson, 87, was a charter member of this clandestine group in World War II, joining cause with the French underground and then fighting the Japanese occupation of China.

But as Johnson sits at his kitchen table, medals and documents from that time spread before him, he said the toughest part might have been keeping a lid on everything he did during the war.

"It was such a hush-hush group. We couldn't talk about it when we got home on furloughs. We were advised not say anything.

"I didn't say anything about it for 50 years."

Former U.S. Rep. Pete Hoekstra of Holland said the OSS was critical in proving the worth of intelligence, paving the way a few years after the war with establishment of the CIA.

"It laid the foundation," said Hoekstra, who presided as GOP chair of the House Intelligence Committee from 2004 through 2006.

Hoekstra said those like Johnson and the agents that followed deserve special notice, since "many of these people serve anonymously. And they die anonymously."

As West Michigan spent the Memorial Day weekend recognizing those who gave their lives for their country,

Hoekstra said it's worth remembering that sacrifice doesn't always wear a uniform.

He helped Johnson secure his award in 2009 of the French Legion of Honor medal, that nation's highest civilian award. He also earned a Bronze Star and several other honors.

"Very seldom do we hear about their successes at the time they happen. For a lot of these folks you may not hear about the impact they had until 20 or 30 years later."

Secrecy was about the last thing on Johnson's mind when the Grand Rapids Central High School graduate enlisted in the Army in February 1943. He was disappointed to be assigned duty as a medic, fearing he would sit out the war "on bedpan duty" at some hospital far from the front lines.

Then he spotted a notice on a bulletin board.

"They were looking for volunteers for dangerous duty with a short life expectancy. That sounded like something that could be interesting," Johnson recalled.

President Franklin Roosevelt established the OSS in June 1942, to collect and analyze strategic information and to conduct special operations not assigned to other agencies. It was the first time a single group encompassed everything from espionage to covert action to counterintelligence.

"I had never heard of it," Johnson said. "I didn't really know what I was joining."

Johnson and some of the OSS recruits ended up at Congressional Country Club outside Washington for their initial training in weaponry and tactics. The trainees virtually tore up the layout with their weapons and explosive practice. "We ruined the course," he said.

In May 1944, Johnson was shipped to northern Africa for parachute training, completing 11 jumps before he was sent to England for commando training. There he honed his weapons skills and learned a variety of ways to kill another man.

In August 1944, he and two dozen other OSS members jumped out of B-24 bombers about 1:20 a.m. into German-held southern France, guided by signal fires set by the French underground.

Their first mission: Capture a nearby hydroelectric plant held by a relatively small German force.

An OSS colonel got word to the German officer in charge he had a large body of men prepared to seize the plant by force.

"He said, 'You either leave by morning or we're going to take over,'" Johnson said.

The Germans left.

"That mission couldn't have gone any better."

A couple of weeks later, Johnson and his OSS comrades coordinated a hit-and-run ambush by the underground of what turned to be a division-sized column of German troops, tanks and trucks.

"We hit them with everything we had," Johnson said. "There was a lot of lead flying around."

Johnson and two others got separated from the group as it retreated, but they were able to rejoin them after spending a night in the field.

There were other such missions.

"We blew up bridges, blew holes in roads, anything we could think of to cause havoc."

By the end of September, the invading Allied forces had taken southern France from the Germans.

It was time for another mission.

"As soon as the Americans had overtaken us, we had to get out," Johnson said.

Johnson was back home for a 30-day furlough, where he gave only vague descriptions of what he had been up to.

By January 1945, he was in India and headed over 1,200 miles of the Burma Road for China. The OSS group spent several months training Chinese commandos on tactics for resisting the Japanese occupiers.

In July 1945, 200 OSS troops parachuted into the rice paddies of central China. Their mission: Disrupt the supply of rice back to Japan.

"I never thought we would live through the Chinese operation because we were so easily identified," Johnson said.

They were sent as "advisers," Johnson said, their orders prohibiting them from taking part in combat.

Their role was further complicated by a growing civil war between nationalist forces and communist forces led by Mao Tse-tung.

"We carried a lot of Chinese money with us. You bought intelligence. You bought loyalty," he said.

The war ended with the Japanese surrender on Aug. 15, 1945, and Johnson was finally home by the end of the year.

By war's end, the OSS had trained resistance forces across in both the Pacific and European theaters, conducted sabotage operations and even used its operatives to penetrate Nazi Germany.

In 1947, President Harry Truman assured that the OSS legacy would continue with creation of the CIA.

Given his background, it's no surprise Johnson took particular satisfaction in the role the CIA played in tracking down bin Laden to the compound in Pakistan where he met his death.

"It's exhilarating to know what we started is still in effect. Of course, things are more sophisticated now. They gave us a handgun and a rifle and said, 'Here's a map. Go after them.'"

Made in the
USA
Lexington, KY